CREDIT UNIONS

Jack Dublin

CREDIT UNIONS

theory and practice

Wayne State University, Detroit, 1966

*Grateful acknowledgment is made to the Michigan Credit Union
Foundation for financial assistance in publishing this volume.*

CONTENTS

Now we have arrived at the waterhole! We who are poor have always paid back twice what we borrowed. Because we were dying of thirst we had to agree. Now a new waterhole is coming to Mipa. When we borrow we will be drinking with our neighbors and for a decent fee. We must be grateful for this opportunity and use it well.

> *. . . So spoke a farmer in Tanzania when the Mipa Credit Union was organized.*

PREFACE

In 1963 with my family I left the United States to live in a country that existed for us only as a strange name on the map of Africa: Tanganyika as it was called then; Tanzania, since 1964. A few people in this newly independent African republic had become interested in credit unions and my job was to encourage, teach, and help those people and their government to start a credit union movement. The Tanganyika Project was truly an experiment in people-to-people cooperation.

Like most experts who have had their eyes opened by overseas assignments, I had much to learn from those I was supposed to teach. I learned that it is far from easy to explain the simple truths of credit union philosophy in meaningful terms rather than cliches and high-sounding phrases, and it is hard work to translate theory into universal examples of credit union practice. Not that the concepts of cooperation and the Golden Rule are new to Tanzanians. They are building a nation around "Ujamaa" the Swahili word that embraces the meanings of brotherhood, unity and cooperation. Their questions were about money—how to get it, how to use it, and how to unravel its mysteries.

Just before coming to Africa I had completed a study for the Michigan Credit Union League on central banking, stabilization, and share insurance that attempted to answer the same questions for Americans. The idea for a book began to emerge, a book that would provoke discussion if it could not provide all the answers, for people who want to know something about the mastery of their own money. What started as elementary lessons in credit union theory and practice thus became the framework of this book.

I have tried to develop the thesis that ordinary men and women like those who make up the credit union movement have the ability to pool their savings for their own best interests in institutions which they control, to understand the financial statements of their joint undertakings, and to decide the direction they want to go in their national and international affiliations with other people doing the same thing.

The great challenge today is to merge the resources of individual credit unions and their organizations in a central bank. In developing the thesis, the logic for this step and the possibilities for its realization are indicated.

I wish to acknowledge with thanks the information in all the books, pamphlets and periodicals listed in the bibliography. Roy Bergengren's book *CUNA Emerges* was invaluable in providing historical references, as was *Credit for the Millions* by Richard Giles. My warm appreciation goes to Cecil Crews of the Michigan Credit Union League for the multitude of materials on money, banking and credit he has accumulated into "bite-size" readings. I am indebted to CUNA International, Inc., CUNA Mutual Insurance Society, and the Bureau of Federal Credit Unions for statistics and current data issued in their various publications.

Special thanks are due to Father John Lavoie, Director of the Social Training Centre at Nyegezi, Tanzania, who encouraged me to record the 1963 lectures delivered there; to my son Mark David Dublin who prepared the first manuscript from these lectures; to my wife, Selma, whose steady advice helped immeasurably to clarify my expressions; to the readers of the manuscript whose helpful criticism guided me in making revisions; and finally to those who shared with me their interpretations of the events of the last twenty years in the North American credit union movement.

The book would never have materialized had there not been the opportunity to live with the people of Tanzania in the early days of their independence. I am deeply grateful to all of the people on the African continent who were so kind to us, and to the credit union people of Michigan and Saskatchewan for their understanding of the needs of others.

JACK DUBLIN
Moshi, Tanzania
March 24, 1966

I

Principles and Practices

Introduction

A credit union is a cooperative, designed to provide its members with efficient, inexpensive savings-and-loan service. Like every other cooperative, credit unions must base their operations on certain principles. In this first chapter we shall discuss these principles, and the ways in which a credit union can apply them to its everyday operations.

Membership

Although a credit union deals only with persons who make up the scope of its membership, the foremost principle in its membership policy is to extend service to as many as possible within its scope of membership. A credit union should not try to become an exclusive organization to which only a privileged few people may belong. Rather, it should aim at becoming an organization which includes and helps as many people as it can.

Of course, most persons would like to belong to a group which limits its membership to people of good character, which excludes those who have been in trouble with the law or who have fallen into low repute in one way or another. But if a credit union restricts its membership so that no "undesirables" can become members, it may very well place itself beyond the reach of those who need it most.

The kinds of need a man may fall victim to are not always those which his neighbors consider respectable or proper.

Often, an otherwise well-behaved man will turn to drink or theft out of sheer desperation. For such a man, as for all kinds of unfortunate people, the credit union has a duty to extend help so that he may become a respected citizen of the community, therefore it cannot turn its back upon those whom the community considers outcasts, so long as these people honestly wish to be helped.

There are other types of people whom credit union members often hesitate to admit to membership in their credit union. People who have worked hard to build the credit union may look with contempt on the man who applies for membership with no other purpose in mind than to borrow money. Likewise, dedicated members may be irked when a man applies for membership who has known all about the credit union for months or years, but has waited to join until some kind of emergency occurs and he cannot find help anywhere else. The question is, should such a man be accepted?

It has been estimated that one fourth to one half of all credit union members in the world joined their credit union with only one intention: to take out a loan. But, once members, many of these people have become hard workers, saving in the credit union and working for it, as well as borrowing money from it. For many people who join a credit union thinking they are joining only to borrow money, the loan acts as an inducement for them to become active credit union members.

Who will be a stronger supporter of the credit union than a man whom the credit union helps in time of extreme need? Whether or not a man has shown any previous interest in the credit union, the credit union may make a devoted worker out of him if it helps him when he really needs help.

In other words, "moralizing" has no place in credit union membership policy. No one benefits when a credit union simply turns its back on someone who asks for help, neither the credit union nor the unfortunate man, whatever his previous behavior or intentions have been. On the other hand, credit unions often find their strongest supporters among people who have learned first-hand that the credit union really is in operation to give help where help is needed.

Does all this mean that the membership of a credit union

must risk its savings in the hands of untrustworthy people? Not at all. Members must keep a careful eye upon those they elect as officers. Likewise, members must exercise a great deal of caution and concern in lending credit union money. The funds must be carefully protected and accounted for. But because it is a credit union, the organization often must go out of its way, though not so far it will endanger members' savings, to extend help to those who need it. While credit union members surely do not need to make officers of people they do not trust, they should include in their membership even the village drunkard if he asks to join. After he becomes a credit union member, the undesirable may be encouraged to reform; in any case, the credit union has a duty to try.

Another principle of credit-union-membership policy is to try to include every member of the family, not only the men of the household. In many communities, women traditionally have been assigned an inferior position, with the men making all of the important decisions. And in many countries, contract laws forbid any organization to lend money to anyone under the age of eighteen. But women, children, and youths can and should be included in membership to as great an extent as possible.

The leaders of many countries have recognized the importance of bringing intelligent and able women away from the cooking pots and into community life. In any community there are potential leaders among the womenfolk, with many valuable ideas; these leaders and their thinking must not go to waste if the community is to take the greatest possible advantage of its resources.

What holds true for growing countries and communities holds especially true for credit unions. No credit union can afford to overlook any potential leaders or workers, consequently to overlook the women of the community would be a serious mistake.

And, speaking practically, who is a more logical credit union member than the lady of the house? She knows from experience how and where money needs to be spent; since she must supervise buying the children's clothing, pick up the family's food, and see to it that the house is kept in good repair, she probably has plenty of experience in handling money. On the other hand, a working mother has the same potential as a working father for credit union membership.

Experience in the United States has shown that, as the economy of a country develops, the wife gets more and more control over the management of the home, largely because the man of the house is too busy earning a living to be concerned with the details of family finance. It appears, therefore, that if the credit union is to keep pace with the demands of any community, especially in a newly developing country, it has no choice but to make room for the women.

Although contract laws in most places say that anybody under eighteen years of age is too young to contract for a loan, the fact is that many youngsters in this age-group do have financial problems. Many people under the age of eighteen work at least part time. And, regardless of the contract laws, there are many ways in which youngsters can fall into debt. Is credit-union service really forbidden to everyone below the age specified in the contract laws?

There are ways in which credit unions can help people below the legal contract age. In the United States, a parent or some adult friend or relative who is a credit union member may open a joint account with the minor who wants credit-union service. Credit union personnel can give advice to persons of all ages. Adults may contract as co-makers for loans on behalf of minors. These are ways in which a credit union can serve minors.

The credit union's duty to help young people is clear. The credit union is in business to give help where people need it, and people below the legal contract age often need more financial help than their elders. Giving special assistance to young people is a good investment for the future of any credit union. Should the credit union show someone how to use his money wisely when he is young, he may remember the advice for the rest of his life. And should a credit union allow young people to participate in credit union activities, the experience of running a democratic organization is also likely to last. Early credit union experience can be valuable in many ways, and the credit union ought therefore to make it available.

Often, an organization of one kind or another will want to open an account in a credit union. What are the requirements in this case? The way most credit union charters are written, the credit union can usually accept any organization composed entirely of people who would be individually eligible for membership in the credit union; if the credit union has a charter for the members of a parish, for instance, any organization of members of that parish is eligible for an organizational membership in the credit union.

An organizational membership entitles the organization to one vote only. Generally, the members of the organization vote among themselves to decide how that vote shall be cast in each credit union balloting.

Organizations become credit union members for the same reasons that individuals do. If the organization has some extra money in the treasury, the members may decide to invest the money in the most convenient credit union rather than locking it in a strongbox or hiding it in the treasurer's mattress. Like an individual, an organization may find itself in need of a loan from time to time. Credit union service is as attractive for organizations as it is for individuals, especially if the members of the organization are all credit union members themselves, hence every credit union probably will receive a sizable number of applications for organizational memberships.

Should organizational memberships be encouraged? The answer is yes, because an organization's funds represent the savings of a group, wherefore its saving habits tend to be more regular and stable than those of individuals. An organization also has wider resources for repaying loans than do most individuals. Records show that organizations usually make good credit union members.

In brief, then, a credit union's membership should be as broad and inclusive as legally possible. Credit union membership will not work miracles, but members can help people in trouble by bringing them into the credit union. The credit union must try to overcome traditions which keep capable women from contributing to the credit union and the community. The credit union should do all it can for young people, in the way of financial help as well as in affording experience participating in a democratic organization. The credit union should make service available to organizations within its field of membership. The credit union's chief principle regarding membership is to include as many people as it can.

Saving

The credit union has two purposes: to provide a place where members can save their money, and to provide a depository of money where members may borrow in time of need. If one of these is more important than the other, it is the first.

A man never knows when he will need more money than his next paycheck or his next crop will bring him. Sickness in the family, loss of work, fire, flood, storms, accidents, marriage, birth, or death—any one of a number of emergencies can demand an unusual amount of money. To have any sense of well-being, most men must have some savings.

Saving money is always difficult. In any country, under any economic system, people have a hard time saving money. One of the most important services a credit union can provide its members is assistance in saving their money; moreover a credit union is not just a strongbox: it must provide advice on saving as well as a place to deposit what is saved.

Credit union experience has shown that certain principles make the difficult job of saving easier. The credit union should try to encourage its members to apply these principles to their own saving habits.

Probably the most important of these principles is *regular saving*. Experience seems to show that unless a man gets into the habit of putting money away, he will find it very difficult if not impossible to save any money at all. On the other hand, if a man does develop the habit of regular saving, he will find that his savings seem to accumulate faster than he had expected. Of course, saving regularly does not make everyone rich, but it is generally the people who have saved regularly who have at least some money on hand when they need it.

In some places, payroll deduction or check-off plans have been instituted. Under these plans, the employer agrees to withhold a certain amount of money from the man's paycheck each pay period and deposit it in the credit union.

Although plans like these make regular saving easier, they are not absolutely necessary; people can develop the habit of saving regularly on their own account. The credit union should encourage them to do so. A credit union with a small treasury at the end of its first five years of operation which represents five years of steady, regular saving is actually running a healthier operation than a credit union with a large treasury which was mostly deposited in the first few months of its existence.

Another practice credit union members should cultivate is that of saving "off the top of the pile." A man should put aside his savings before he spends any of his paycheck. People who start spending their paychecks as soon as they receive them often find that they have no money left to save. The payroll-deduction plans make it easier to save money before spending, as well as to save regularly. But, once again, credit unions should encourage good saving habits with or without these plans.

Granted that good saving habits are more easily practiced in some places than in others. Many people such as farmers and craftsmen are not paid wages or salaries. Many farmers must depend on one crop for most of the year's money. But people who have any income at all can save regularly. A few coins saved every week may accumulate into enough to buy a bottle of medicine at the end of several months. No matter how large or how small the amount, it is important that money be saved regularly, and that money be saved before spending can begin.

Most credit unions find themselves hard pressed to attract savings, but once in awhile a member will bring in a sum of money so large that credit union officials may be afraid to accept it. This raises the question of whether or not credit unions should accept large amounts of money.

In some places, credit union laws do not permit one member to own more than a certain percentage of the money in the credit union. The reasoning behind such a rule is this: if one member owns most of a credit union's capital, the credit union depends on him. A democratic organization can not depend on one member.

But in many places credit unions still may be faced with the question: What should a treasurer do in such a case?

First of all, the treasurer should make absolutely certain that the man who has brought in the money understands the credit union. The treasurer should sit down with the man and go over in detail exactly what the credit union is and what it is not, to clear up the misunderstandings which so often occur. People can have any number of misconceptions about credit unions, and this places the credit union under obligation to explain its function to everyone who invests money in it. There are benefits in credit union membership. There are also risks. All aspects should be clearly understood. Before the credit union accepts money from anyone, it must be sure it is accepting the money in good faith.

Once the treasurer is sure that the man understands the credit union, he should accept the money if it is legal to do so. The credit union may have to hire a guard and incur other expenses to protect the money. But the credit union must have the courage to accept it. If the credit union is to gain the confidence of the community, it must show that it has confidence in its own ability to protect and handle large or small amounts of money. Once a credit union is in business it must be willing to accept as much responsibility as it is allowed. Otherwise it is avoiding its duty to offer service to all those who ask for it, even at the cost of some inconvenience.

To fulfill its principle of helping people who need help, the credit union should learn to watch for tell-tale signs. Certain saving practices indicate mistaken saving habits. And poor saving habits often are the harbinger of financial trouble.

Credit unions often see a member bring in a small amount of money one day and withdraw it the next. A man who does this may not understand the problems he raises for the credit union. Or he may be in debt, and forced to use any extra money he has to pay interest somewhere else.

Repeated deposits and withdrawals are a headache to bookkeepers. They use up a treasurer's time. Although other savings organizations might just tell the poor saver to stop bothering them, a credit union must try to find the root of the trouble.

Someone must counsel the man on his saving habits. Perhaps the treasurer can do it. Perhaps another member can sit down with the man and find out what the trouble is. However it is done, someone must try to help the man solve his problem; this is the credit union's responsibility.

Ownership

Everyone who invests money in a credit union is an owner. Comparatively few credit unions let members both buy shares of ownership and deposit money, constituting a loan to the organization. But most credit unions simply say that when a man brings in savings he automatically buys shares. So everyone who saves in the credit union is a part-owner of the credit union, his liability limited to his shares subscription.

Profit corporations assign votes by shares; a man has as many votes as he owns shares. A credit union does not operate this way. No matter how much or how little money a man has invested he has only one vote.

The reasoning behind the credit union's policy is this: first, a democratic organization cannot be run with "weighted" votes; since a credit union values democratic control, it must allow all members equal voting power. Secondly, the amount of a man's savings is not necessarily an indication of their importance to him; one percent of a wealthy man's income may be more than fifty percent of a poor man's income. Thirdly, those with the most money are not necessarily those most capable of running the organization, therefore credit union government is strictly one man = one vote regardless of how many shares a man owns.

Loans

Credit union loans must be tailored to fit the needs and capacity of the borrower, not so as to earn for the credit union in interest charges as much of his money as possible. Keeping this principle in mind, the credit union should plan every loan carefully with the borrower. Because the primary purpose of a credit union loan is to help the borrower, this planning session is a most important part of the lending process.

When counselling a borrower, the treasurer should help

him decide how much money he really needs to borrow. Between them, the borrower and the credit union adviser should discuss just what the money will be used for. The credit union representative should not lecture the borrower on what he should or should not buy. He should try to help the borrower plan so that he can get his money's worth of whatever he does want to buy.

Together, the borrower and the credit union adviser should also consider the borrower's income. They should calculate to see if the borrower can reasonably afford to repay the loan on his income. They should calculate to see just how the payments may be arranged so that the loan can be repaid in the shortest amount of time possible, and to fit in with the borrower's anticipated income from wages or crops.

Prompt repayment of loans is a principle for both the credit union and the borrower to remember. The borrower is expected to honor his obligation and to repay the loan according to his agreement. The credit union is not in business to make a profit from its loans. Neither is it expected to incur expenses for collecting loans. When borrowers repay their loans promptly, they can expect to get help when they need it. When they take longer to repay than is absolutely necessary, or when they cause expense and trouble to the credit union, everyone in the cooperative is hurt.

A credit union should never make a loan that obviously cannot be repaid. What the credit union should do is to help the borrower negotiate a loan that he can repay. Should the credit union grant loans that will take long terms to repay? Very often, a large, long-term loan is the only kind of loan that will really solve the borrower's problem. If a man is in debt to a merchant, or a moneylender, for instance, the fastest way to solve his problem, and the least expensive way for him, is to borrow enough money from the credit union to repay his debts completely. As we shall see, it will probably be much easier for him to repay the credit union than any other creditor. But the credit union should make sure that the borrower fully understands the terms of the loan, and exactly what it will cost him. And the credit union should do all it can to make sure that the loan can be repaid eventually, even if it takes years.

Members must be encouraged to be honest with the credit union if it is to help them borrow money so that they derive the greatest benefit possible from their loans. The credit union must build up a feeling of trust between itself and its members, but building up mutual trust is not easy.

Through years of bad experience with authoritarian employers or government, people in some places get into the habit of keeping the truth from anyone in a position of authority. To run a democratic institution like a credit union, people must be shown that honesty is now in their own best interest.

To encourage members to be honest, credit union officials must prove that they can be trusted absolutely. To this end, credit union members must be especially careful to elect only people who they know can keep confidences.

The credit union officials who handle loan counselling must also be men who will not moralize to members who come in with problems or belittle a member for getting into trouble. The official whose job it is to counsel members with their loan problems should be someone who will treat everyone who comes to him with dignity, and who will be careful not to tear down another man's self-respect no matter what kind of trouble he has got into.

Credit unions have been very successful in this area. There have been cases where people will tell their credit union treasurer things that they would not tell their priest.

The credit union's loan policy, then, should be liberal insofar as it can be. The credit union should not look for excuses to disapprove loans. Nor should it grant loans carelessly. It should look for the best way to make the loan, so that the borrower benefits as much as he can, and so that the credit union is assured of getting its money back.

Interest

To pay its expenses, provide reserves, and pay dividends, the credit union must collect interest on its loans. In most cases, credit unions find that they must charge the maximum interest allowed by credit union laws, 1% per month on the unpaid balance of every loan. This amounts to 12% a year simple interest. The aim is to reduce the cost of interest to the borrower, because 12% is not a low charge even though it is reasonable when compared to the interest charged by other lenders—banks, 18%–24%; loan companies, 36%–42%; loan sharks, 1,040% or more.

After a credit union has been in operation long enough, there are ways in which it can reduce the actual amount of interest it charges; interest refunds will be mentioned shortly. But if it is to keep operating, a new credit union must generally charge as much interest as the law allows, and it must let its members know that it is doing so. Truth in lending is a credit-union principle.

If a credit union admits that it is charging these interest rates, will members still borrow from it? If they can, they almost certainly will. Because at a true 12% a year on the unpaid balance of a loan, credit union loan service is almost always demonstrably much less expensive than practically any other loan service to the same group of people under the same conditions. Credit union loans may be expensive. A man may have to go out of his way to pay back his credit union. But most likely he will not be able to borrow money at less actual cost anywhere else.

In many developing areas of the world, credit for the average man is hard to come by at any price. Many banks and loan companies have little confidence in the ability of a farmer, a worker, or a civil servant to repay a loan. So the people in these places are cut off from the legally chartered lending institutions.

But there are times and places where a man must borrow money. If his crops have failed, a farmer must find money somewhere if he is to eat, let alone buy seed for the next planting. If sickness occurs in a factory-worker's family, and if the company he works for does not provide him with medical care, he may find that his wages are not large enough to cover the medical bills. So credit can be a matter of life and death. People in these circumstances must borrow somewhere.

In these situations, people often go to a local moneylender. Almost every community in the world has someone who makes his living by lending money to his neighbors. And these people rarely limit the interest they charge to anything like the credit union's 12% a year on the unpaid balance of a loan. Because a loan from a moneylender is comparatively easy to get, and because the terms seem reasonable, people do not realize how expensive this kind of loan service is.

A moneylender usually will offer such terms that a man may borrow five dollars for a week if he will pay back six at the end of the week. One dollar for the use of five for a week is 20% interest per week. There are 52 weeks in a year. Interest at this rate amounts to 1,040% per year, or nearly 87 times what the credit union will charge.

This example is not the worst by any means. In many places, particularly among the people who can least afford it, debt is carried through several generations, so that grandchildren may have to pay off the debts of their grandparents. People who have to borrow money under conditions like these are quick to see the advantages of borrowing at credit union interest rates.

One of the principles of a credit union is to reduce its interest rates as soon as it can. Some credit unions charge lower rates on all loans or loans of certain types, such as new auto loans or loans fully secured by shares. Other credit unions reduce rates by paying an *interest refund.*

At the end of every fiscal year, or other accounting period, the credit union simply credits a certain percentage of the interest which a member has paid on loans for that year back to his share account. In this way, the credit union gives back some of the money he has paid as interest.

Some credit unions have been paying as much as a 50%-interest refund for years. If a credit union collects the maximum legal amount of interest, one percent per month on the unpaid balance, and pays a 50% interest refund, it has cut its interest rates to 6% a year.

A credit union should build up both its funds and its experience with bookkeeping before it starts paying an interest refund. The credit union's first concern is to have enough income to give service to its members, the best service it can.

Dividends

At the end of each fiscal year, most credit unions pay their members a *dividend* on their savings. If the credit union members vote themselves annual dividends of 4%, then a member who has $100 in his account for one full year will have four dollars added to his savings. Generally, dividends are added on to the member's share account although he may always elect to receive cash payment.

The practice of paying a dividend is a carry-over from profit businesses. It is possible that in the developing countries where new ideas are being tried, credit unions will be doing away with the practice completely. Why?

First of all, the dividend does not serve the same purpose for the co-operatively minded credit union member as it does for the profit-minded business investor. A profit corporation pays dividends to investors because that is their only reason for investing. People invest in a credit union mainly for saving and loan service. Very likely, most credit unions in developing countries could attract the same number of members with or without paying individual dividends to each member.

The most important reason for doing away with individual dividends is that the money which the credit union pays out in dividends could buy more for the group if kept together than it could divided up among the individual members.

Suppose a credit union has a thousand members, with $25 each in their accounts. If the credit union pays a 4% dividend, each member will receive one dollar at the end of the year. One dollar cannot buy very much. So, in effect, the total dividend of one thousand dollars will simply disappear into thin air shortly after the dividend is paid.

But, if kept together, the one thousand dollars could be used for some project to benefit the entire group. With one thousand dollars, the group could buy schoolbooks, or building materials for a school or meeting place, or even pay for a well to provide drinking water. Instead of paying a dividend, a credit union might reduce its interest rates, making loan repayments easier.

If the members of a credit union want to vote themselves a dividend, they have every right to do so. But it might be better credit union practice to use the money for some other cooperative-group purpose.

Operations

A credit union is a business. It must adopt the business principle of running its operations as economically as possible.

Because a credit union is in business to help its members does not mean that the credit union can waste its money or the time of the volunteer officials. The credit union should watch its funds very carefully, to see that expenses are controlled, and the work is planned efficiently. The treasurer has a responsibility to see that all of the money is correctly accounted for.

A credit union must depend largely on volunteer help, which raises some problems. Volunteers may think they need not extend themselves, because there will always be someone else around to do the job. Volunteer organizations often forget that the time any one volunteer can be expected to put in is limited, since he has to earn his living at some other job. Some volunteers are married women, who have families to take care of, and others are students, who have schoolwork to do.

Each credit union official, whether he is a volunteer or a paid employee, should have a definite job with definite working hours. In this way no one will be taken advantage of, and the credit union can be sure that the work will get done.

A credit union can generally tell whether or not it is running an efficient operation by watching its *expense ratio*. The expense ratio is the proportion of expenses to income earned on loans and investments. A credit union should keep its expense ratio below fifty percent. For every hundred dollars of income the credit union should spend not more than fifty. Multi-million-dollar credit unions often run closer to a forty percent expense ratio. They can afford certain techniques and machinery which are not available to a smaller credit union, and so they can become more efficient.

Just as any other business organization does, a credit union must plan for its future. The credit union should prepare a budget at the beginning of each year, estimating its income so that it can decide how its income is to be apportioned.

The credit union must not leave anything to chance; it must plan for as many of its expenditures as it can.

In all of its operations, the credit union must work efficiently, to give its members the service for which they joined.

Association with Others

While profit businesses often can afford to compete among themselves, credit unions cannot. The cooperative principle must govern the relations of credit unions to each other and to other cooperatives.

The economic difficulties facing cooperatives of all kinds, and especially credit unions, are so formidable that these organizations must unite if they are to survive at all. Formation of credit union leagues or federations is in line with the credit union principle of one for all, all for one.

CUNA International, Incorporated, is the world-wide organization of these leagues which exist in many countries. The eventual aim of the credit union movement is a world-wide federation of credit unions, with member organizations in all nations, pooling not only their economic resources but their experience, their education, their inspiration, and their enthusiasm.

The principle of increasing economic power by uniting individual funds is especially pertinent in the case of the credit unions themselves. The power of $5,000 in the treasury of one credit union is very small compared with the power of $100,000 pooled in a bank owned by twenty credit unions the same size. Organization of specialized institutions for this purpose has started, but there is much work to be done even in the highly developed countries where credit unions are strong. One of the most important immediate objectives in the U.S.A. is the legalization and formation of a credit union bank or reserve system for credit unions. It is not unusual for credit unions to deposit their money in other financial institutions which use the profit from credit union funds for campaigns against the credit union movement.

Make no mistake. Uniting credit unions costs money, and the cost of affiliation with others must be borne by each individual credit union. In figuring its budget, each credit union should plan to set aside some of its funds for this purpose while still maintaining its fifty-percent expense ratio. Perhaps some of the credit union's individual interests will have to be set side.

Gaining strength through uniting with other credit unions and cooperatives may seem less important to a new credit union than many other attractive projects. Credit union leaders may feel that association with other credit unions can be put off for a long time. But in reality, unity is literally a matter of life and death for the credit union movement and for each individual credit union.

II

Who Can Organize a Credit Union

Introduction

A credit union is a basic form of cooperative in which people can help themselves economically and learn to work together. It would seem therefore that almost every kind of group could use the services of a credit union. From that assumption it is all too easy to assume that every group which understands the benefits of having a credit union should want to organize one.

The most dangerous assumption of all is that because the credit union plan is so simple most groups automatically understand how it works and what is required of the members.

No person who is to have the responsibility for organizing a credit union can afford to make any such assumptions. He must remember that this activity must be an expression of interest and dedication by the people involved, and that the success of the credit union depends on how far they are willing to go in providing leadership, learning to operate it, and using its services. None of these essentials can be imposed from the outside upon the credit union or the group it serves. They must arise from within the group.

The organizer must work with the group to make sure a credit union is needed and desired by them, and to be certain that they realize their obligations to themselves, to their government, and to the credit union movement. The organizer must help the would-be leaders of the new credit union to understand fully what is involved in running a credit union before any organizing is done at all.

Thinking about Organizing

Whether the organizer finds a receptive group to hear his story, or whether he is invited in to advise a group that has already picked up some information on credit unions, he should remember that his responsibility is to help the group, not merely to organize another credit union. He is not a public-relations man whose purpose is to convince everyone that credit unions are miraculous organizations which can remedy every conceivable problem. The good organizer is an adviser whose job it is to see that if a group does decide it wants a credit union, a good credit union will be established.

IMPORTANCE OF GROUP LEADERS

Group activity invariably calls for leadership. In the case of credit unions the leadership must come from within the group. There is usually no great difficulty in identifying the leaders—they are the individuals who have taken the time to inquire about the credit union plan or have come forward in support of the idea after their interest has been aroused. If the organizer knows the group well he may be justified in searching out individuals whom he knows to be leaders for an active role in the credit union. Otherwise, he is well advised to leave this entirely to the people who make up the group.

By helping the group leaders to define their problems, and to see how the credit union can provide some of the answers, the organizer will accomplish two invaluable services for them. First, their understanding of the work to be done in solving their problems will help them to see to what extent a credit union can succeed. Second, knowing what is expected of credit union officials—integrity, hard work, little or no remuneration—will help them to decide individually whether they really want to start a credit union in which they might logically be expected to accept an official position.

WHAT CREDIT UNION IS AND IS NOT

With this in mind, the organizer should discuss with representatives of the group just what a credit union is, and what it is not; he must try to help them understand what it can be expected to do for them, and what it cannot be expected to do in relation to the problems they have identified. I would venture to say that conceivably every group could use the services of a credit union, but not always for the purposes that seem apparent to them.

The organizer should be careful not to give a group the impression that the credit union is a cure-all for their various economic and social ailments. For instance, social and economic conditions may be such, and the poverty so acute, that people may resort to pawnbrokers for cash to meet daily needs. Credit unions can help but they alone cannot solve the deep-seated social and economic problems of a nation.

However, the organizer will often recall instances, from his own experience or through reading, where credit unions have amazed their own members by demonstrating the power for economic and social good that can be generated by ordinary people working together. Father Coady, the dynamic priest who planted the seeds of credit unions and other co-operatives among the fishermen-farmers of Nova Scotia, said, "The people can do ten times what they think they can do." Truer words were never spoken.

Make the Most of the Group's Abilities

A credit union sometimes enables a group to mobilize their savings and put those savings to work in ways that seem almost miraculous. Imagine the amazement of the African farmers who, with an average cash income of Shs. 700 ($100.00) a year, watch their combined savings in a credit union with 200 members climb to Shs. 70,000 in a two-year period, and see the new roofs, the farm improvements, the school fees paid for through loans from their own savings!

But there is nothing really miraculous about what the credit union does. All it does is to help the group make the best of what they already have. A credit union cannot provide anything in the way of money, honesty or willingness to work for people who have neither the possessions nor the potential for these things. If there is no honesty in the group, the credit union cannot make the people honest. If they are unwilling to help themselves, the credit union cannot turn everyone into a hard worker. But by demonstrating what happens when people work together in a cooperative, with a well-thought-out plan, the credit union can help most people to put their savings to work for them and—perhaps even more important—help them develop their own abilities to manage a business enterprise.

So far, the movement has come across few, if any, groups who have absolutely nothing with which to start a credit union. Even people who do not use a money system of exchange could start a credit union using food, tools or staples of some kind as their savings to be deposited or loaned out. Likewise, there are not many groups who lack the honesty needed to run a credit union. For a community to exist at all the people in it must be able to trust each other. And to survive at all, they must be willing to work. Hence, credit unions continue to flourish in the most unlikely surroundings.

COMMON BOND

One important element in credit-union organization is that the people to be served, the potential members, should all have something in common with each other. This is called their common bond. The words "common bond" describe the tie that binds the group together, so that they know something about each other and understand each other's problems. Having a common bond helps to make for a successful credit union because there is already existing in such a group some of the feeling of mutuality, loyalty, and trust that eventually must be built into their relationship with the credit union.

Is there any reliable test to determine whether the group has this common bond? No, not in the sense that any such test could predict for certain whether a group will eventually succeed or fail with their credit union.

However, there are three types of common bond generally accepted to classify groups in North America where credit unions have been organized on a large scale. There is the *occupational* common bond in which all of the group work for the same employer, or do essentially the same kind of work even if they do not have the same employer. If all of the group live in the same community or locality they have a *residential* common bond. And if they already belong to some other organization, such as another cooperative, or labor union, or church, they have an *associational* common bond. It is possible for the same group to have more than one common bond. And it might be impossible for a group that is perfectly worthy of having a credit union to fit all of its people into one of these classifications: occupation, residence or association. The organizer therefore must be flexible and resourceful in helping the group to decide how they will define their common bond on a workable basis, if they do not fit into one of the three categories. Fortunately, the common bond of residence should serve for almost any group. For example, farmers living within a given trade area around a village or town where they come to buy and sell have at least two common bonds: occupation—they are in the same kind of work—and residence—they live in the same area.

City workers face a more difficult problem, as they do not always work in a group sufficiently large to operate a credit union under one employer. They may find a common bond in their labor union, or church, or some other type of association. Or they may have to find their common bond in the community where they live.

More and more, experience is showing that the best common bond is the integrity and purposefulness of the group. If they have a real need for a credit union, and a good understanding of how to satisfy that need with a credit union, they probably have the ability to solve the problems of leadership, communication and morale that all credit unions must face. This combination of need, understanding, and desire to form a credit union is a fourth type of common bond.

PLANNING AHEAD

Only a handful of leaders can be counted on to take the initiative in organizing a credit union. But those few leaders can help to circulate information, to answer questions, and to eliminate doubt about the new organization. At some point they must help the group to decide whether they do or do not want to start a credit union. The agreement is rarely unanimous. Sometimes ten subscribers are required to sign an agreement that they will buy shares in the credit union, and that is sufficient to get started. In some cases it may be necessary to get more signatures, or even to raise a given amount of share capital in advance, before the government will approve the registration of the credit union or issue a charter to it.

The organizer can help these leaders to plan ahead, knowing that each step toward the actual operation of their new credit union can arouse increasing enthusiasm and interest. Study materials, including standard credit union bylaws, are usually obtainable from the credit union league or from government. Their studies should not, however, be so prolonged that they lose sight of the jobs waiting to be done. First is the charter (or formation) meeting at which the group are to meet with the organizer, and if possible with the government officer who will help them to meet the government's requirements for getting their charter. Second, there will be an organization meeting after the charter is approved (or registered) by the government. Specific arrangements must be made for both of these important meetings.

Preparations can be made also for operating the credit union. By the time a determined group of leaders have made up their minds to organize a credit union, it can be reasonably assumed that they will succeed. The successive steps that follow their decision should build more and more enthusiasm among the entire group, until the peak is reached on the day the credit union declares itself organized and ready to do business.

Some very practical questions must be answered. Perhaps the roads are poor; if so, how will the members get to the charter meeting and the organization meeting? Perhaps the group is composed of taxi drivers who work at irregular hours. How will they make their share deposits and get their loans? Suppose there are no telephones. How will the officers and members communicate with each other? Farmers always have some work to do throughout the day and during certain periods they cannot leave their farms. How will their credit union conduct business on a regular basis? The organizer can help the group to list some of these questions on paper, and as the answers are worked out they can be written down, thereby creating a question-and-answer educational bulletin that can be posted in a central place or reproduced and distributed. With this kind of guidance, a beginning credit union can make advance plans for office space, the hours of business, safeguarding the money, and many other foreseeable problems of operation.

ORGANIZER DOES NOT HAVE ALL THE ANSWERS

The organizer is wise not to assume that he has all the answers. He must turn the problems over to the people who are going to have to solve them for themselves, and he would do well to hear what they decide to do about their own difficulties. Credit union operation is based on the assumption that people are usually the best judges of what is best for themselves, and the organizer can give a group confidence in their own ability to make the decisions that they alone can make.

Charter (or Formation) Meeting

After the group has discussed and solved some of the foreseeable problems, it is time to think about actually starting the credit union. They must start making preparations for the charter meeting. At this meeting those interested in having a credit union will review credit union principles and practice once again to make sure they understand what a credit union is, what it is not, and how it will operate. At this meeting they will prepare bylaws and an application for charter to be approved or registered by the agency of government that has this responsibility. Often a fee is charged for registration or issuing the charter, and this must be collected to accompany the application. There should be a nominating committee elected or appointed to nominate a slate of officers to be elected at the organization meeting which will be held after the charter is approved.

Usually a large attendance is not expected at a charter meeting. This meeting is a serious study session, requiring close attention and serious thought. The review of the proposed bylaws alone may require extended discussion, sometimes lasting for several hours. However, in some localities the people are accustomed to meeting in large groups for such purposes. If the entire group wants to attend the meeting and participate there is no reason they should not. In any event, the law usually requires that there be a minimum number of subscriber signatures on the application for charter, usually not more than ten. Many groups do not consider holding their charter meeting until they have substantially more than the minimum number of subscribers for the charter application. If the group can get more subscribers without delaying their timetable excessively, so much the better. At least the minimum number of subscribers required for the application should be at the charter meeting. If this attendance cannot be assured, the group had better do some more thinking and discussing before they try to organize a credit union.

Including Government Officer

Besides the leaders of the group, another important person that should attend the meeting is the government officer who recommends approval of the charter, or his representative. This officer should really be informed as soon as the group start thinking about organizing a credit union, because his support, his understanding, and his encouragement will help the credit union greatly after it gets started. The credit unions that are his responsibility can build a good relationship with him by involving him in their organizing efforts from the start. It is a good idea to have regular communications with him, in writing if the opportunities for personal contact are insufficient. As he is probably a busy man it may not be practical to invite him to any meeting until the group are sure that there is enough interest as well as reliable leadership to take definite action toward the establishment of a credit union. By the time the group plan the charter meeting they should be sure enough of themselves and their plans to make attendance at the charter meeting a justifiable use of the government officer's time.

Order of Business at Charter Meeting

Inasmuch as the credit union is in the process of formation the purpose of this meeting is to get agreement from a representative number of people in the group on the plans to organize a credit union. This is a serious decision and those attending the meeting will get the opportunity to ask all the questions they may have been accumulating while the proposal has been under discussion. Open discussion is welcome. A good charter meeting will be conducted with as little formality as possible, but a chairman will be needed to keep the discussion moving, a secretary should record the decisions, and there should be an agenda, including:

1. Election of temporary chairman and secretary
2. Explanation of the purpose of the meeting
3. Introduction of the government officer, the league representative, and other guests
4. Remarks of the government officer, the league representative, and guests
5. Review of the principles and purposes of the credit union
6. Review of the proposed bylaws
7. Decision on whether to make application for charter
8. Collection of charter (or registration) fee
9. Election of nominating committee
10. Election of a trustee or key man to accept payments from prospective members

The government officer will provide forms for the application in advance of the meeting, or will bring them with him, and may wish to oversee their completion. Standard bylaws are usually available from his office, or from the league, and it is not necessary to employ anyone to assist with the preparation of these documents. If the group believe that the standard bylaws do not fit their needs, changes may be possible either by agreement with the government officer at the time of application, or later on after the credit union has had some experience on which to base a request for a bylaw amendment.

Preparing Bylaws

Credit union bylaws in many countries reflect a continuing effort to improve the working rules of these organizations, and each day new experience brings new ideas for improvement. Ordinarily the bylaws provide for amendments to be approved by the credit union membership, or by managing committees or board of directors; and usually no amendment becomes effective until it is also approved in writing by the government officer who has supervisory authority. Unless there is to be an important or substantial change from the standard bylaws, the organization of the credit union should not be delayed while prolonged negotiations are carried on with government.

Not all countries have laws or ordinances specifically drawn for credit union organization and operation. Some countries have a cooperative law under which it is possible to devise bylaws suitable for credit unions. Where no enabling law exists it becomes a matter for negotiation with the government, and bylaws can be based on those of some other country where conditions are believed to be similar; these bylaws should be very simple, in fact the simpler the better.

Selecting Nominating and Arrangements Committee

At the charter meeting the group should choose a nominating committee to line up a slate of prospective officials to fill the elective positions in the new credit union. The prospective members of the credit union who will vote for their first officials at the organization meeting are under no obligation to elect the slate of the nominating committee, but it is necessary to know that there will be some people willing to accept positions as officials by the time the organization meeting is held. At the charter meeting one of the group should be elected to head the nominating committee, and this person should not be the organizer. If the group cannot find other leaders, and must come back to the organizer the first time that they are called upon to produce one of their own leaders, they show a serious weakness that eventually may lessen their chances of having a successful credit union.

Charter (Registration) Fee and Other Expenses
of Organizing

At the meeting, or immediately thereafter, the committee must collect the money for the charter or registration fee, if one is charged, usually from payments towards entrance fees and shares of the first subscribers. Money will be needed also to pay for the initial supply of bookkeeping forms. A group may have a fund built up from previous activities or a sponsor who wants to donate the money for these initial expenses to help the credit union get started. Most groups will experience no problem in collecting this money from prospective members, especially if recognition is given to the charter members. It should be explained in advance of the charter meeting that it is an honor to be one of the charter members of this organization that may someday be one of the most important institutions in the community.

If the charter meeting is successful the group will have a good foundation for its credit union by the end of the meeting. It will have its bylaws and its application for registration ready to be submitted to the proper officials. And it will have elected a group of people whose job it will be to choose possible candidates for officers, to keep up the interest of the group and to make all the preparations necessary for the next important meeting, the organization meeting, when the whole group will gather to begin building the credit union.

Organization Meeting

After the charter meeting, the committee elected there will have much work to do in preparing for the organization meeting, the meeting at which the new credit union will elect its officers and enlist many new members.

The organization meeting must be planned very carefully, because it will be most people's first experience with the new credit union, and it will be important to make a good showing.

While the government agency in charge is considering the group's application for a charter the committee should be constantly working among the group to keep interest in the credit union from dying out. Especially in new countries people want things done immediately, and tend to lose enthusiasm for a project when there is long delay in getting started. Since it may be at least a month or two before the government registers the bylaws or even gives a definite answer on whether or not the credit union stands a chance of being chartered, the people in the group may lose their patience and forget about the credit union. The committee must not allow this to happen.

The committee must use all the imagination it can muster to keep the group interested in the credit union idea until the government can finish considering the application. It must find other people in the group who are also highly enthusiastic, and put them to work making speeches at any gathering place, handing out literature, holding meetings, and even accepting savings, provided that sufficient preparations have been made for keeping this money safely, for keeping a record of who has contributed savings, and for giving a proper receipt to each saver.

The committee must be extremely careful to safeguard the money. At the start, savings of only a few dollars can give the credit union a tremendous boost and encourage many other people to join. But the loss of someone's money in the early stages can deal the credit union a tremendous blow before the organization meeting has even been held. It is best to authorize only one person to accept payments and issue receipts. He must keep detailed records of every payment received.

Likewise, the committee should be careful to see that its workers, in their enthusiasm, are not misleading the people. Nobody should join the credit union with any illusions, if the committee can possibly help it.

NOMINATIONS

The committee should devote itself to its primary job of nominating candidates for the official elective positions including the officers, in preparation for the organization meeting. In nominating for the board of directors or managing committee it must consider carefully who will be the best qualified people to fill the positions of chairman (or president), vice-chairman (or vice-president), secretary, and treasurer. It must then make sure that these people are willing to serve.

Unfortunately, the most conscientious, capable people in every group are often hesitant to serve as officials. Where this is the case, the committee must do its best to encourage these people to accept nomination.

The important thing is to have a slate of suitable candidates ready on the day of the organization meeting.

HANDLING MONEY

In planning for the organization meeting the committee must make careful preparations for handling any money the group want to bring in. If the committee and its workers have done a good job there will be a number of people who will want to pay their membership fees and buy some shares on that first day, at the organization meeting.

Many countries have good banking facilities and a source of credit union stationery. Having bookkeeping supplies on hand to keep track of the money brought in at the organization meeting, however, may present a problem. In some countries, there is no source of readily available credit union bookkeeping forms and equipment.

In the event that no official bookkeeping supplies are available the committee will have to make up its own set of bookkeeping forms to record the receipt of money. Ordinary slips of paper with duplicates provided by carbon copy, signed by the member whom the committee assigns the responsibility of handling the money until the treasurer is elected, and by the treasurer himself after the organization meeting, can serve as receipts. A neatly kept pad of pencil-lined paper can be used as an emergency cash book, a cross-reference to the cash receipts from which the figures can be copied as soon as the bookkeeping supplies can be obtained.

Adequate preparation for keeping the money safely should not be left to chance either. The committee must make definite plans for a safe place to keep the credit union's money, both before and after the organization meeting. If a local bank is not available, it may be that the credit union will want to open an account with a bank in a nearby city. If so, the committee should send a representative to the bank to discuss such an account before the organization meeting is held.

Until the collections are deposited in a bank, they must be protected. Perhaps the committee can find a reliable safe to store the money in. Perhaps the money can be entrusted to a man who has a permit to use a weapon. Or the local police may be willing to provide protection. The important thing is that the committee make careful plans to see that the credit union fund is fully safeguarded before the organization meeting is called.

CALLING ORGANIZATION MEETING

When all the preparations have been made, and when the government has told the group that their credit union will definitely receive its charter, it is time to call the organization meeting.

As this is supposed to be a meeting of everyone who is eligible for membership in the credit union, it is a good idea to plan for a very large group. Publicity should be widely distributed, and the committee would do well to put the most imaginative and creative people it can find into the publicity campaign.

Although the group should be made to realize the gravity of the business at hand, the affair should be made as attractive as possible. A community might make the organization meeting a holiday affair, with dancing and refreshments after the serious business is finished.

The credit union wants to get as many people as possible to come to this meeting, and if the credit union workers have been doing a good job since the time of the formation meeting, there will be more chance of having too large a crowd than of having empty seats.

THE ORGANIZATION MEETING GETS UNDERWAY

Once the meeting is underway, once the group is gathered in the appointed meeting place, what is the business to be considered? First a temporary chairman is chosen. After the announcement of the registration of the bylaws the first business on the agenda will be the election of the officials who will hold office until the first annual meeting of the members.

The nominating committee has prepared a list of the people who they think will do a good job and who they know are willing to serve as officials of the credit union. Now it is up to the members of the new credit union either to approve these people for the offices or to elect someone else who they think would do an even better job.

Every potential member can be invited to vote, whether he has contributed any money or not. Thus the first elected leaders can be truly representative of the group who will be members during the coming year.

The committee should not feel insulted if the group do not elect everyone whom they have slated. The job of the nominating committee was merely to suggest a list or slate of people who are willing to serve. Other members of the group may have in mind different persons they think will do a better job than those suggested by the nominating committee, and upon whom they think they can depend more fully. It is up to the group to choose its own officials.

If the committee has done a good job the group will realize the seriousness of the responsibility that goes with a credit union office, and will not elect anyone unreliable or inefficient. Long before the meeting, in their speeches and conversations, the committee and its workers should have made it clear to the potential members that at this meeting the credit union will be electing officers to manage the members' money for an entire year.

Before they come to the organization meeting the group should be made to realize that it is electing leaders who should be able to learn their duties, and who will be absolutely reliable. This is not the place for insincere office-seekers.

Generally, people know who can be trusted with responsibility. If the members really want an able but reluctant member to be an official they can usually persuade him to take office. The nominating committee should have few worries about the group's ability to come up with a set of leaders for its credit union.

At the organization meeting, after the elections, people will start to bring in their money. We have already discussed the necessity for proper preparation and orderly procedure in collecting this money. Possibly someone will even apply for a loan. The managing committee will be present, after just having been elected. It is possible for the authorized credit-union officials to approve and grant the loan right then and there, and it would be a real achievement for the new credit union to make its first loan on the first day of operation.

By the time the organization meeting is over the credit union should be firmly established as a working corporation. It will have its own elected officials and, it is to be hoped, enough capital to make a good start. It will be a legally constituted body, given certain rights and certain limitations under the law. It will be given the right to sue and will accept the liability to be sued. It cannot be dissolved now, except by the legal procedure for dissolving a corporation. All of the group have taken on a large responsibility in organizing their credit union to give themselves the means to do many things they could not have done as individuals.

What Organizer Should Accomplish

If the organizer has been successful he will leave behind him a working credit union capable of handling its own affairs and solving its own problems and willing to take responsibility for its own actions.

He will have left the group with a leadership of its own who may not know all the answers and will be frank to say so but who have basic confidence that they have something good in the credit union, which they will be able to run by themselves.

If the organizer has left the group totally dependent on himself or some other outsider as the expert and sole arbiter of credit union affairs, he has not done a good job. For one thing, the whole credit union plan demands that the group be fully capable of running their own affairs. For another, the volunteer organizer has other work to do. Even if he is a paid league or government employee the organizer must move on to get other credit unions underway, and he cannot afford to be returning constantly to a group he has helped to organize. To be successful the organizer must leave the new credit union standing firmly on its own feet.

The successful organizer will have introduced the new credit union officials to a friend in the person of the government official responsible for credit unions in the area, the man who will work with them on a regular basis and perhaps more closely than any other outsider.

Sometimes volunteer organizers may find it easier to work with league personnel than with government supervisors. Generally, government staff who take the time to help organize credit unions are both dedicated and competent as are league workers.

It is quite natural for the organizer—be he an unpaid volunteer, or a paid league or government employee—to take a personal interest in his "baby." Consequently he may make some harsh judgments about the ability of others involved in the organization efforts. An understanding attitude can help to avoid judgments of this kind, and may create lasting friendships. Even paid employees may be still learning about credit unions when they attend organization meetings. What better time to learn how volunteers, credit union leagues, and government all can learn together and work together to guarantee the best possible credit union service to the people?

Again, if the organizer has been successful the group will understand perfectly well that they are handling their own money, not something loaned to them or given them by the government, the church, or some wealthy man. They will realize that it is up to them to protect the money in their credit union as their own.

Before he leaves the organizer should give the new credit union the address or phone number of someone other than himself whom they can rely upon for advice. A credit union that has been operating well for several years would be an excellent source of practical information for a new credit union. The group should be ready to stand on their own feet, but there is certain to be advice which the group will need, and which only experience can give. The new credit union should know where it can get such advice.

Finally, if there is a credit union league in operation the organizer will, it is hoped, have helped the new credit union to join the league, to lend strength to the entire credit union movement, and to receive further encouragement from it.

If the organizer has accomplished these things by the time he leaves he will have been instrumental in the successful beginning of a credit union and he will enjoy the satisfaction of having helped others to create an organization of lasting importance.

The Steps in Organizing a Credit Union

1. THINKING ABOUT ORGANIZING
   —*What can a credit union do for a group of people?*
   —*What is a common bond?*
   —*How will the credit union operate?*

2. CHARTER MEETING
   —*Getting help from the government and league*
   —*Reviewing what a credit union is, and is not*
   —*Preparing bylaws*
   —*Selecting a nominating and arrangements committee*
   —*Charter fee*

3. IMPORTANT STEPS BETWEEN DATE OF CHARTER MEETING AND ORGANIZATION MEETING
   —*Keeping interest alive*
   —*Accepting money readily and keeping records*
   —*Nominating committee makes arrangements for*
       Handling money at the organization meeting
       Bookkeeping supplies
       Keeping the money safe

4. ORGANIZATION MEETING
   —*Call to the meeting*
   —*Conducting the meeting*
   —*Elections*

5. WHAT ORGANIZER SHOULD ACCOMPLISH
   —*The new credit union is self-reliant*
   —*The credit union leaders consider the government officer their friend*
   —*The credit union members understand their responsibilities*
   —*Membership in the credit union league*

III

Cooperative and Community Developments through Credit Unions

Credit unions are not "cure-alls" for the problems of any society any more than they are for all the problems of a country. What credit unions can do is to mobilize the human resources of a country by giving people a method of solving their own problems. Although this chapter pertains more especially to conditions in developing countries, the principles it sets forth are applicable to the most advanced countries where minority groups have recently acquired political and economic liberties.

Credit Unions and Economic Freedom

In every newly independent or developing country the people are highly impatient and insistent that conditions be improved immediately, in the belief generated during a long period of looking forward to independence, or to major social, political, and economic change, that all of their problems will disappear with the old system.

People who believe that economic freedom will accompany national independence or newly won political freedom forget that independent countries and democratic governments have the same problems as they did before they achieved independence or democracy. The only difference is that they can no longer depend on foreign governments or omnipotent officials to solve the problems of whole populations. The old problems of poverty, ignorance, and disease will still be there.

Free men must work to overcome these problems themselves.

Leaders of many countries are trying to impress upon their people the idea that economic freedom can be gained only through their own hard work, not by way of gifts from other nations. They point out that, no matter how much foreign capital comes into a country, the people will never have the economic freedom they want until they are capable of managing their own affairs, of making their own decisions and taking responsibility for them.

Under authoritarian governments, foreign or domestic, people often become accustomed to having help brought to them from outside, without their having much to do with it. The administration runs the government, the schools, and the public utilities without asking the help of the people. It imposes the restrictions which it thinks are necessary. Although people may object to these restrictions, and hope to be rid of them, they should not forget that, under any authoritarian system, the government also assumes a large degree of responsibility. Unfortunately, people are not so eager to accept this responsibility themselves as they are to be rid of the restrictions.

This is where credit unions are important. For a credit union to function properly, it must teach its members to think and act for themselves, instead of waiting for some official to make their decisions for them. The experience in self-reliance which credit-union members gain can be transferred to other areas of their lives, including government and the management of other cooperatives. In this way people learn to be self-reliant, the first prerequisite to gaining economic freedom.

Credit Unions and Cooperative Principle

One of the most valuable services credit unions can perform is to demonstrate the value of the principle of cooperatives. Most of the newly developing countries are providing cooperatives a friendly climate in which to grow. Their governments and people accept the cooperative principle. There are no well-financed, well-organized anti-cooperative groups, as there are in some of the older countries. Just the same, the people of the newly developing countries must be shown that cooperatives really work before they will invest in them or work with them. They must see that the cooperative principle is not just a pleasant idea but a sound economic philosophy on which to build the economy of their country.

Credit unions are ideal showplaces for the cooperative movement of any country. There are many people who will not have the same opportunity for identification with the cooperative idea which farmers or fisherman may have. City life tends to be competitive, and a man with a job in the city may feel that cooperatives are not very important. The cooperatives he finds in the city may be few and far between. A credit union of city employees might serve to give these people a new look at cooperatives. The credit union may also give them some organization to identify with, to replace the tribal or village life they left behind them when they came to the city.

Most important, a great many city dwellers desperately need credit union service. People who go to the city from farm or village often discover that, while city jobs pay well in comparison with farm work, the cost of living in the city is so high that a man may find himself in debt even if he is earning more in a month than he saw in six back home.

A credit union can show a man that people can be trusted, an important concept for cooperators to remember. Not everyone can be trusted all of the time. But when working among their own neighbors, and handling their own and their neighbors' money, most people will be honest. A credit union in operation can show this very effectively.

A credit union puts a premium on trustworthiness because it makes use of people's concern for their own money. Because credit union members are dealing in their own money, they will be very careful where they lend it. To receive a credit union loan, a man will have to show that he will probably pay it back. People are usually on their best behavior when they are dealing with their friends, relatives, and neighbors in any case. A credit union cannot turn many criminals into honest men, but it can encourage honesty, and such encouragement usually pays off.

Some people do not believe it is possible for anyone to be trustworthy, but even these persons, when they see that their loans are being repaid, come to understand that, under the right conditions, most people really can be trusted. Thus the credit union performs a valuable service to the cooperative movement by showing that the cooperative principle of trust is an effective one.

Even more important than teaching its members to have faith in each other, the credit union can teach them to have faith in themselves. All over the world people are reluctant to handle too many of their own affairs. They have either been convinced or have convinced themselves that most important matters are beyond their understanding. They believe that control of many aspects of their lives, even personal ones, are best left to officials and experts.

This is especially true with savings and loans. People tend to feel that money matters are best left to bankers, and that bookkeeping and accounting are just too far above comprehension for the average man ever to exercise any authority over the way his money is managed.

But when people see that their fellow villagers or fellow workers can pick up credit union bookkeeping after a few simple courses, and when they see that their credit union can be made to function through their own efforts alone, they begin to realize that they are much more capable than they thought they were.

A credit union is a simple organization. People can acquire the knowledge it takes to run a credit union very quickly. For one thing, managing money is not as difficult as some people think. Neither is running a democratic organization. Many people doubt their own ability to do either, but if they can form a credit union, very likely they will learn that they can do both.

As it has already been stated, credit unions are operating examples showing that the cooperative principle is an effective principle, thus they encourage the development of other cooperatives, and other forms of democracy.

Laying Foundation for Better Cooperatives

As well as showing that the cooperative principle works, credit unions can help to make sure that the cooperatives themselves actually develop into effectively functioning organizations, and that they will continue to have a favorable climate of government and public opinion in which to operate.

As we have seen, the governments of many new countries are firmly dedicated to the idea of cooperatives. Many governments actually have established cooperatives in their countries.

Too often, these organizations are not run as true cooperatives; their operation is controlled by their officers rather than by their members. Many bitter criticisms have been raised against these government-sponsored and government-controlled cooperatives. Critics say that a cooperative should be run by the membership, not by an outside agency.

Unfortunately, many of these controlled cooperatives had to be established that way because so few members knew anything about running a cooperative. The government, in a hurry to meet popular demand, could not afford to delay the cooperative program until enough people had been trained to provide satisfactory democratic leadership.

Government-sponsored cooperatives cannot go on this way forever. They cannot remain under government control. They cannot remain the only cooperatives a country has. Most governments which have instituted controlled cooperatives do not want them to remain controlled any more than do the members. A government does not have the time or the money to supervise every detail of the country's economy, besides which the people will develop an increasing interest in conducting their own private as well as public affairs. And both government and citizens realize that a great many more cooperatives will be needed to develop the economy than the government can either establish or control.

Leaders from among the members must be trained to take office in the government-sponsored cooperatives, and to organize and govern other cooperatives started by the people themselves without the government's taking the initiative. Credit unions can provide the training-ground for this leadership.

Because of its simplicity the credit union is an ideal training ground for practical experience in credit union membership and government. Being the president, vice-president, or treasurer of a credit union requires integrity and a sense of responsibility, but it is not really a complicated job.

The skills of bookkeeping, for instance, are not hard to master. The relatively small sums a credit union treasurer will have to deal with during the first few months of operation provide the opportunity for him to get the feel of his job. Once he has learned and practiced the basic skills, he will be ready to handle increasing amounts of money. After a year or two, he may be expert enough to handle the accounts of a much larger and more complex cooperative than his original credit union.

Not only does the credit union provide training for officers, but also it stimulates members with the idea of running their own cooperative. It allows them to acquire the experience of membership in a true cooperative, not a puppet organization managed mainly by the government.

Because the credit union deals solely and directly with their own money, the members can easily absorb the idea that the credit union is their own, which they must manage by themselves; and once they get used to running it they will not find it difficult to transfer the same idea to the other cooperatives, either marketing cooperatives, cooperative stores, or whatever form of cooperative may emerge. Hence a credit union provides excellent practical training for cooperative management and membership at the same time.

There are other concepts which are important to the cooperative movement as a whole, and which credit unions can teach their members.

The idea that the credit union's money is not the property of the officers is a concept which must be learned if any cooperative is to succeed. Too often a cooperative treasurer will come to believe that, because he has contributed his time and some money, and because the money is in his care, he may from time to time make use of it, as if it were all his own. To prevent this, the credit union can render itself and the cooperative movement a real service by impressing its officers and members with the fact that the money belongs to the group and is not to be put at the disposal of any one person without the consent of either the group or its representatives acting according to the rules laid down by the group and the government.

Unless a credit union makes this principle clear to its members and officers it cannot function long. Once the principle has been impressed upon them, they will remember it and carry it with them to their other cooperative associations.

The principle that everything in the cooperative's possession must be accounted for is another important principle that can be learned through the credit union. The credit union accounting system is not difficult to grasp and, in working with it, the members can easily get the idea of keeping careful track of everything received and spent. As in any business, accurate accounting is important in every kind of cooperative from consumer store to brick-making project.

The concept of cooperation with the government is another important principle credit unions can instill. People in every country tend to resent their government to different degrees. In a developing country resentment may reach such proportions that it becomes a serious obstacle to national progress. People sometimes feel that the government is there merely to punish them when they break rules, and is of no use to them when they need protection or help.

In most countries the government cooperative department or ministry will send inspectors to make sure the credit union is functioning properly. Members of a larger cooperative probably would have little contact with the inspector, whereas credit union members can see the inspector at work. They will come to understand that he is an ordinary citizen, like themselves. They will see that he is not there to get the credit union into trouble with the government, but to help keep it out of trouble. They will come to appreciate his knowledge of bookkeeping and the law, and to accept him as a valuable source of information on the operation of their credit union.

If the members and officials of cooperatives resent government inspectors, and if a great deal of ill-will develops between government and cooperative personnel, the progress of the cooperative movement can be severely hindered. On the other hand, the credit union can provide the first-hand contact that can help to bring understanding between people and government, thereby helping the cooperative movement.

One more service the credit unions can perform for the cooperative movement as a whole is to inculcate in the next generation, and every generation to come, understanding of the cooperative principle and the cooperative movement, and their importance to the country.

A credit union member may pass on to his children his belief in the credit union. Children are naturally observant and, since the credit union will be at work so close to their families, they will have the opportunity to observe a cooperative in action from childhood onward. They should be familiar with it by the time they become old enough to take part in the activities of the credit union or other cooperative.

In addition, a credit union may decide to use part of its funds to support scholarships for members to be trained as teachers, who may become skilled in teaching about cooperatives, as well as other subjects such as reading and mathematics, all necessary to the development of the cooperative movement and the country as a whole.

Also, children and young people may borrow money with the aid of their parents, although they are not eligible to deal with the credit union by themselves. And everyone, young or old, may save his money in a credit union.

In these ways credit unions can assure the cooperative movement a firm base for the future as well as the present.

Looking Ahead

It is difficult to say exactly what shape the cooperatives of any country will take. The possibilities for different types of cooperatives are practically limitless. Already there are cooperative-type consumer stores, insurance societies, marketing societies, and even electric-power companies. In the future, no one can say how many industries and how many areas of national life will become cooperative. It is safe to say, however, that whatever other cooperatives are organized there will always be a need for credit unions. Why shouldn't credit unions be the financial center of other cooperatives owned by their members? Why shouldn't there be a credit union available to accept investments from other cooperations —or make loans to them?

As a country advances, it will need more and more trained technicians, teachers, and administrators. The government can finance the training of some of these people, but many will find that they can fill the government position they want only if they are already possessed of some training. There will be an increasing need for credit union loan service to enable people to finance their own training. The practical experience in cooperatives which credit union members receive also will stand them in good stead.

Credit unions are beginning to offer programs to students, whereby secondary-school and university students may go to school part time and work part time at the credit union, gaining experience in bookkeeping and the handling of money.

The future looks very bright for cooperatives in many developing countries. In countries where credit unions have been started, the credit unions, as emphasized above, have the responsibility to see to it that the cooperative movement develops to its full potential. How should they take this responsibility?

First, they must express their dedication to the concepts of service and brotherhood.

Second, they must practice these concepts, to prove that they work.

Third, they must impress upon their members the idea of personal responsibility for personal affairs, financial and otherwise. They must teach their members to stand on their own feet and make their own decisions.

Fourth, credit unions must show their members that the government is a friend to be trusted and treated honestly, not an enemy to be outwitted.

And fifth, they must induce people to put the cooperative principle to work in as many other fields as possible, once they have seen it work in the savings-and-loan field.

If credit unions fulfill these responsibilities, they will be performing a very important function in the cooperative development of their country.

IV

Credit Union Management:
Putting Theory into Practice

Credit union management is basically the democratic government of a democratic business organization. In addition to knowing the skills and principles necessary to running a business, credit union management involves knowing how to run an establishment whose final authority rests with its entire membership. In its management as well as in the rest of its operations, a credit union depends on cooperation between people. This chapter explains the methods of putting credit union theory into management practice.

Management and Its Fellow Members

It is important to remember that the credit union is owned and controlled by its members. They are the final authority in all decisions on the operation of the credit union, within the limits of the law. The decision of the members at the annual meeting is the final word on how the credit union is to be run.

To carry on the everyday business of the credit union, of course, the members must delegate their authority. Usually they elect a board of directors, a credit committee and a supervisory committee. In some countries these officials are known as the managing committee. It is their responsibility to set daily credit union policy, perform all of the duties required in making loans, keep track of employees, and do whatever else is necessary to keep the credit union running properly. For the rest of this chapter we shall refer to the entire group of elected officials as management.

A healthy, friendly, democratic relationship between the rank-and-file members and management is absolutely necessary to the well-being of the credit union. The members should be encouraged to take an active part in credit union elections. The officers and the rest of management should feel that they have the respect and confidence of the other members who elected them.

Under no circumstances should management treat fellow members as a flock of sheep to be herded, or as if management had all the answers while the other members had none. It is a great temptation to officials in all organizations in any country to adopt the attitude that they are justified in doing exactly as they please to carry out the responsibility they have been given regardless of the feelings of the people who gave it to them.

It is easy for an official to bring himself to believe that the reason he was assigned leadership responsibility is that he is better qualified to handle it than the person who delegated it to him and, because he is better qualified, he need not accept suggestions or listen to any criticism from those who elected him.

An official who reasons this way will often view the average credit-union member as just one more hindrance in the performance of his job when in fact the real strength of the credit union lies in the personal interest shown by the members. It is never a good idea to brush off a member and his suggestions.

Management should remember that all of its authority comes from the vote of the other members. Elected officials will do well to treat the other members as fellow members, which they are.

Democratic Participation

Democratic participation is important to any credit union. If the members fall out of the habit of participating the actual control of the credit union will gravitate to an increasingly smaller group of persons. Finally, the majority of the members will have no control over the use of their money, and one of the primary purposes of the organization will be defeated.

Management should encourage the members to offer ideas and suggestions at the proper meetings and through daily communication. *Democratic participation* are the key words of healthy credit union management.

How is a policy of encouraging democratic participation actually put into effect in the operation of a credit union?

First of all, management must see to it that there is a constant flow of information between the other members and themselves. By way of newsletters or other forms of bi-monthly, monthly, or even weekly reports, the management must let the other members know what is going on in their credit union's operations. The members have a right to know if their credit union is being managed in their best interests.

Likewise, management should encourage members who have suggestions to come forward at any time and offer them. One official may be specially assigned to handle members' suggestions and to seek out the opinions of those who are not members. Very often a credit union member may be able to point out something important that management has completely overlooked. Members often come up with useful suggestions for simplifying paperwork, for attracting more shares and loans, or for improving annual meetings. A simple suggestion for changing the business hours may be just what is needed to bring in the man who was always too busy to join the credit union.

Management cannot be everywhere or see everything. By listening to other members' suggestions and to people within the field of membership who have not joined, management gives itself a valuable source of information it needs to perform its job with the greatest effectiveness.

Annual Meetings of Members

The annual membership meeting provides the greatest opportunity for management and the other members to exchange ideas and for everyone to make known his views on credit union policy. The annual meeting should be carefully planned with this goal in mind.

The annual meeting is the most important meeting of the credit union's year. At this meeting members decide how they want their credit union run. They elect their management for the next term. They offer their views on what the credit union should do and how it should do it in the next year.

At the annual meeting the different divisions of management (board of directors, supervisory committee, credit committee, and educational committee if one exists) all report to the members on their operations for the year. These reports should be factual and to the point, preferably in writing and if possible supplemented by charts where visual aids are needed during the discussions.

There must be time for the members to discuss policy. The members should be given enough printed information on each point of discussion to enable them to vote accurately and sensibly. Motions from members should be encouraged.

At the annual meeting, as well as throughout the rest of the year, there must be a free and open atmosphere and a friendly relationship between management and the other members. Management must do a little extra work to encourage such an atmosphere, but that atmosphere must exist if the credit union is to function well. Thus, the extra work involved will be justified.

Members' Responsibility to Management

Now it is time to consider the other members' responsibility to their fellow members who are the management. For every case where a breakdown in relations results from abuse of power by management, you will probably find at least one other case where the jealousy, unfounded suspicion, noncooperation, or other unreasonableness of the general membership has ruined the cooperative atmosphere of the credit union.

People everywhere tend to resent authority. People in authority impose rules and punishment. They collect taxes. To some extent, they tell a man how he is to live his life, consequently people tend to resent those they classify as authority.

Whether the authorities are acting in the majority's best interests or not, resentment still remains. It reaches some fairly high proportions when the people have little or no control over the authority that runs things for them, no matter how good a job it does, especially where such a situation has existed for a long time.

In many organizations in every country the relationship between the governing body and people who are governed is one of distrust. Members of primary societies of marketing cooperatives suspect that their officials are not acting in the best interests of the general membership. Students are constantly wondering whether or not the school authorities are trying to avoid giving them their money's worth in education, supplies, and food. Even members of some religious groups are reluctant to follow rules of their church because they are not sure that their church leaders observe these rules themselves.

Some of this distrust is probably justified. A great deal of it probably is not. The fact remains that it exists and that it is a major obstacle to the development of any organization.

Mutual Trust Is Important

Lack of trust can ruin a credit union in a very short time. Members who do not trust each other will not lend to each other; a vital part of the credit union machinery breaks down then and there. If great distrust develops between the general membership and individual officers or the rest of management, people will hesitate to entrust their savings to the credit union, thus paralyzing the other major part of credit union machinery, the savings mechanism. Once these two processes break down the credit union can be ruined.

Even if the financial damage is slight the healthy functioning of the credit union as a democratic organization will suffer. Members will not work with or cooperate with officers they do not trust; thus it may be that the entire management of the credit union will end up in the hands of these officers, leaving a tremendous gap between management and other members.

How can credit union members guard against distrust such as this? The best way to do it is to elect persons they trust in the first place. The surest way for this dangerous distrust to get started is for the majority of the members to sit back and let a minority elect the management, then start distrusting management because they did not elect it themselves. Silly as it sounds it happens exactly that way far too often.

If people take a genuine interest in elections the chances that an untrustworthy person will get elected are relatively small. People who have worked with new credit unions estimate that the members will elect the right man to office 99% of the time if they are told exactly what the office requires.

Constructive Criticism

After the management is elected, the members owe it a generous amount of trust as a matter of fairness. The members have elected these people to carry on the business of the credit union. They must let them know that they trust them to do so.

This does not imply that blind trust makes for good credit union operation. The members must watch to make sure that the credit union is being run in their best interests at all times.

Management should understand that the members are watching them to correct them if they should happen to make a mistake, although they should not be made to feel that their fellow members are watching them to catch them *when* they make a mistake. There is a difference. In the first instance, the atmosphere is one of cooperation. The members assume that their management is basically honest and capable and that it will make only a few mistakes, and honest ones at that. In the second instance, the atmosphere is one of hostility. The members assume that, being officials, their management is basically incompetent or tricky and that the general membership must constantly keep an eye on management like a policeman watching a known criminal.

If the credit union cannot gather enough cooperative spirit to mold a trusting relationship between management and the rest of the members then it may as well not go into operation at all.

In reality few groups should find it difficult to assure cooperation between members and management if they put their minds to it. The question of trust is stressed here mainly to underline its importance to effective credit union operation.

Common Decency

Management derives all of its authority from the wishes of the majority of the members. The total membership is the boss of management.

But does this mean that every individual member has the right to act as if he himself controlled the whole managing committee? The credit union had better not allow such a situation to develop. Management, we have said, cannot be allowed to brush off the members. Neither can single members be allowed to dictate to management.

Many cooperatives have this problem. Members will come to believe that each official in management is the personal servant of every one of the general membership, and that anyone can burden the treasurer, or any other official, with all kinds of complaints and threats.

Naturally, management subjected to this kind of treatment will simply refuse to serve after a very short while. The credit union must prevent mistreatment of its officials by other members if it is to retain the leaders it can respect in management position.

Every individual member is *not* the master of management. The votes of the membership decide credit union policy, which management must follow. To that extent and no farther is the membership the boss of management. All members have the right to see that management adheres to the policy established by the vote of the membership, but no individual member can decide credit union policy for himself and then try to enforce it on his elected officials.

There are any number of ways in which members can spoil the harmony between themselves and the people they elect. Constant complaints about petty matters, demanding special privileges, non-cooperation with credit union rules, and making accusations of favoritism against officials are just a few of the ways to discourage able people from accepting office.

The golden rule is a good formula for building harmonious member-management relations. You might call it just *common decency*.

It is common decency for an officer to listen attentively and perhaps sympathetically to a member's suggestions or his problems. And it is also good business for the credit union. Cooperatives have a genuine reason for wanting every member to feel that he and his ideas, his happiness, his disappointments, his success, are important. It is common decency for a member to understand the problems that management faces, and to realize that the credit union's elected officials are human beings like himself, and far from perfect.

This kind of golden rule forbids breaking appointments without excuse or apology. It does not permit one man to make accusations about another man without giving the accused person a chance to defend himself, or to know of the charges.

It is, after all, nothing more than the respect people deserve simply because they are human beings with feelings. Credit unions gain dignity and respect in the community as their members show respect for each other.

Structure of Credit Union Management

Management of a credit union is generally divided into a board of directors and several committees. The most important of these include the credit committee, which considers loan applications and rules whether or not loans are to be granted to each applicant, and the supervisory committee, which keeps an eye on all phases of credit union operations, to see that everyone is doing his job properly.

In some countries members are directly elected to the board and to each committee by the vote of the general membership; in other countries the members elect the managing committee as a whole, and allow the managing committee to divide itself into a board and the separate committees.

Once elected management of most credit unions has the authority to appoint other committees as it sees fit. Many credit unions have an educational committee charged with keeping interest in the credit union alive, distributing information about credit union principles in general, and educating the communty in economic and other matters.

Management Functions

Management of any organization consists of certain basic functions. One way to describe these functions is in terms of planning, organizing, directing, coordinating, and controlling. How does credit union management fulfill each of these functions? In this chapter we consider what has to be done by the whole management team, but mostly the board of directors. Chapter 5 will discuss who does it.

PLANNING

Before any project is started somebody has to plan it in as much detail as possible. When the credit union first gets started the new officials should look ahead to make sure that there will be some kind of desk space and basic bookkeeping stationery. Later on management should plan for the time when the credit union will need larger quarters, perhaps a building. Annual meetings must be planned in advance so that the members will all be notified in time for them to make their own plans for attending and so that the meetings will proceed smoothly and efficiently. As the credit union gains acceptance and membership increases, the ability of management to plan well has a decided influence on sound growth.

Nothing just happens anywhere, and credit unions have no reason to expect that their problems will just happen to be solved. This is the work of management; to do as much planning as necessary to keep the credit union prepared for any development, the next year or the next day.

ORGANIZING

After planning the next job facing management on any project is to get things organized so that the plans can be easily carried out. Management performs its first organizing job when the board of directors and all of the separate committees are properly set up, with a place to meet, meeting dates, and an understanding of the job to be done. The board of directors elects the officers: a president, vice-president, secretary and treasurer. Each committee chooses its chairman and secretary.

It is up to the board of directors to organize the business operations by deciding where the credit union will do business, and when. It must decide what the credit union's policies will be, on loans, interest rates, savings, and dividends;

where it is going to send its money for safe-keeping; what employee positions are needed and their pay scales; and anything else that is necessary to the smooth functioning of the credit union.

Perhaps the organizing duties of management can be compared to the building of a machine. They have already made the plans, and the blueprints; from those plans, they set up the machinery of the credit union.

DIRECTING

After the credit union's *machinery* is installed, it is management's duty to direct its operations to see that it works properly. Where there is a decision to be made on credit union policy which is not of great enough importance to require the vote of the entire membership, it is the responsibility of the board of directors, the credit committee, the supervisory committee or the educational committee.

Most decisions on credit union operation are of this kind. Questions of purposes for which loans are to be granted, and who shall receive them, or purchase of equipment, or hiring and dismissing of personnel can be decided by management without the vote of the entire membership.

Some decisions will be made by the committees of management, acting within policy already decided by the board of directors or the membership.

In credit union management direction implies participation. Officials should be prepared to participate in both decision-making and unpaid work needed to start the credit union and keep it going.

The treasurer is usually the general manager, and he often becomes the most powerful member of management. He should be decisive, but he may command so much respect that, within a few months, the rest of the officials look to him for the final decision on everything. Even the credit committee or the supervisory committee may give up authority to him. This is detrimental to healthy credit union functioning.

Management may delegate some powers to individual officers, but its responsibility can not be delegated. Passing the decision-making powers to one official, or to a minority of officials is, in effect, cheating the members out of the total representation they are entitled to. The members elect management to direct operations and they have a right to expect that none of their representatives will default.

Also, just as management must not let one or two officials make policy decisions for all, neither may it load all of its work onto the back of the treasurer or a few members. Management must not allow the treasurer to become its boss, but neither must it allow the treasurer to become a servant. It is good for the board of directors to decide that the credit union office shall be kept clean and presentable. It is better to help the treasurer to keep the office looking nice. A treasurer who has worked until late at night locating a bookkeeping error may know that his office is a mess but he will feel much better about his job if another director offers to help straighten up the office.

As firmly as the other officials let the treasurer know that they have a right to share the policy-making should they let him know that they consider it their responsibility also to share the dirty work, anything from cleaning up the office to locating delinquent borrowers. Willingness to work as hard as the next man or harder encourages others to do their share.

People everywhere respect a hard worker. To be respected as a credit union official, a man must be willing to do hard work. When a man takes a nomination for a post on management he must realize that he will have to work much harder than other members of the credit union, in return for the rewards of personal satisfaction and prestige.

COORDINATING

For any piece of machinery to function effectively the movements of its parts must be coordinated, and credit union machinery is no exception. The officials and committees must direct their efforts so that they are not working at cross purposes, the efforts of one not cancelling out the work of another.

The credit union cannot function well if the board of directors decides on a loan policy that limits loans to a two-year period while the credit committee decides that some loans can be made for longer terms. Caught in the middle, the treasurer would be under conflicting orders until the two official bodies coordinate their policies.

Management should make sure that there are never two men doing a job which could be done by one. Such *duplication* is expensive and may seriously increase the time it takes to get the job done. In a voluntary organization it is not easy to schedule the work of volunteers who have their regular life work to perform ahead of credit union work. Usually the directors and committeemen involved will work out a suitable schedule if they understand what their particular job is and how it fits into the total operation of the credit union. The president and committee chairmen are the chief coordinators for this scheduling.

An important point to remember in coordinating credit union operation is that the board and committees should not be allowed to step over the bounds specifically set for them and arbitrarily assume powers and responsibilities of each other. Since many credit union officials start out with little experience in management the problem of interference by one group in another's work can become a headache.

Naturally, all of the members of management are interested in the well-being of their credit union, and want to see it managed properly. When they see someone else making a mistake their first impulse is to rush right over and say, "You're doing that all wrong. I know how to do it right. Let me show you."

The supervisory committee, for instance, may see that the treasurer is not giving savers proper receipts for their money, or observe that the treasurer is making a loan without the proper number of co-makers. The supervisory committee cannot allow mistakes like these to go unchecked. It is their duty to bring them to the attention of the rest of the managing committee as soon as possible.

But what too many supervisory committee members do in such cases is to walk right over to the treasurer and scold or correct him then and there, in front of the member who is depositing his savings or getting a loan. By taking over the treasurer's job, even if he is not doing it right, they humiliate him for what may be an honest mistake and leave the member in serious doubt about the competency of management in general.

Or perhaps the credit committee will make several bad loans within the space of a few weeks or a few months. It is a great temptation to the rest of the board of directors to say, "You've been lending money to too many unreliable people. From now on, all loans of any sizeable amount will have to be approved by the board as a whole."

In such a case the credit committee will probably answer, "We're human beings and we can make mistakes. If you think you're infallible, you may as well take over all of our work. We're not going to keep on approving loans when you don't really think we know what we're doing." Immediately, the credit union has a fight on its hands, with a great deal of bitterness between the members of management.

Instead of wasting time and money while they feud with each other, the officials can try to understand more about their cooperative relationship and how to do their jobs in the best interests of the credit union.

The board of directors must be sure that the supervisory committee supervises and recommends only within definite boundaries, that the credit committee has enough freedom to exercise the power vested in it, and that every other committee stays within its own bounds.

Does this mean that there should be no calling attention to mistakes, that each group has the right to do just exactly as it pleases, with no checks of any kind? Of course not. But the corrections must be made at the proper time and place, and in the proper spirit. If the treasurer is handing out faulty receipts, or is not complying with the legal lending requirements, these facts should be pointed out to the board of directors as soon as possible. The board should then approach the treasurer, in private, and point out his mistake to him.

If the credit committee seems to be unable to avoid making bad loans, it is up to the rest of management to meet with the credit committee members and say, "Let's see what we can all do, together, to find out what's wrong with our loan policies." Perhaps the fault lies not with the credit committee but with the board of directors who set unworkable loan policies in the first place.

If management does a good job in the area of *coordination,* it will make credit union service more efficient, and will give each member of the management team a feeling of accomplishment and pride in his work.

CONTROLLING

Now comes the matter of management's duty to control operation of the credit union. In what ways can management watch its functioning to make sure it is being run in the best interests of the membership?

SUPERVISORY COMMITTEE

First of all, through the supervisory committee, management can make sure it knows all of the problems and possible faults of its credit union. As we mentioned before, it is the duty of the supervisory committee to check into all phases of operation to make sure that everything is operating as it should.

The supervisory committee must spend some time every month examining the bookkeeping records and minutes of the board and the credit committee, to determine whether the officers and committees are functioning.

It is up to this committee to check the credit union's books and records at least twice a year. At least once a year the supervisory committee should conduct what is called a balance-sheet audit, to make sure that the balance shown on the general ledgers, the figures which go on the financial statement of the credit union, are correct. The supervisory committee should review the work of the treasurer on a selection basis, choosing the records and entries at random for auditing, unless they have time to audit everything. Several times a year they should check some of the passbooks, making sure to complete the verification with the treasurer's records at least every two years.

The supervisory committee checks on the rest of management as well, to make sure that they stay within the law, and to see to it that they keep to the policies which they themselves set.

Checking over the minutes of the board of directors' meetings, they can see whether or not the board has a record of regular meetings, and is adhering to the policies it has adopted.

If the credit committee is granting loans that appear to be uncollectible, it is the duty of the supervisory committee to bring that up to the committee and board of directors.

The supervisory committee must observe everything in the credit union's operations, in short, to help make sure that the organization is following the provision of the law and bylaws which make for safety and growth.

Normally, the relationship between the supervisory committee and the people it supervises is a friendly one. Although nobody really likes to be criticized, most persons are willing to listen to criticism if it will help them to improve their work. The supervisory committee must remember that its job is only to observe and report, not to take any corrective action on its own.

The work of the supervisory committee is important to the well-being of the credit union. It has been observed over the years that individual mistakes in operation, and isolated instances of dishonesty, will not ruin a credit union if they are discovered and corrected, but that repeated cases of mistake or dishonesty not eradicated over the course of time may very well destroy the credit union. Obviously, this function of the supervisory committee is vital to the health of the organization.

Credit Committee

Management exercises another form of control over operations through the credit committee. When a member applies for a loan the division of management known as the credit committee must decide whether or not it would be safe to grant the loan.

The credit committee is free to gather information from every possible source to help its members decide whether or not the loan should be made. The credit committee may speak with the applicant's employer or his fellow workers to determine the applicant's reputation for keeping his word.

It may check with local merchants to see whether the applicant has a good record of paying his debts.

Once the credit committee has gathered as much information as it thinks it needs, it rules on whether or not the loan is to be granted. The decision of the credit committee on loans cannot be overruled by anyone.

BOARD OF DIRECTORS

There are other ways in which management can and should exercise control over operations. The board of directors has the power to meet and act quickly to remedy a harmful situation; in this area, the amount of control it has depends on its understanding of the financial statement.

As a doctor can tell by a patient's heartbeat whether the patient is in good health or not, the board can tell by the financial statement whether the credit union is operating properly. Chaptex VII explains what the financial statement means and how it should be interpreted.

Because only a few members of the board may understand anything about bookkeeping, some directors may allow their attention to wander while the treasurer is reading the financial statement. If this be the case, most of the board will have no way of knowing how their credit union is coming along financially. They will have to take the treasurer's word for it, thus nullifying an important check on the conduct of the treasurer.

The board of directors should consider it a matter of first importance to be sure that all its members can understand the financial statement. Familiarity with the credit union's records is another important control element available to the management committee, perhaps the most important in some situations. A study session with the treasurer will help those who need this training.

Observation by the board of directors is another important control over operations. There are many things which any director can see for himself, without waiting for a recommendation from the supervisory committee.

The condition of the offices, for instance, is usually obvious enough that it can be judged without any great amount of research, and the way the office looks is tremendously important in building people's confidence in the credit union.

No matter how untidy a man's job is he wants to do business in a neat, clean place. He may work on a farm, in a factory or a mine; he may bring in his passbook smudged with dirt or motor oil, on his way home from a day's work; but he still appreciates a bright, clean room in which to do business.

Credit unions often have a problem making their quarters attractive, as all too frequently the only space they can get is space which nobody else wants. But it is part of the control duty of management to see that the office is made suitable for business. It might even schedule a special meeting of all officials, a meeting whose sole purpose will be to make the office look presentable by the time the meeting is over.

At the annual meeting, when it is answerable for its actions to the entire membership, management must see to it that the meeting is run in an orderly manner, so that the members are encouraged to speak up and give their views and opinions, and so that the elected officials begin the next year with a real feeling for what the members want.

The board must see to it that, if the credit union becomes a member of a national or international organization of credit unions, it will be an energetic, participating member. It must exercise its control in that area also, to see that the members' ideas are carried through to the larger organization and the credit union's representatives take an active part in the larger organization's programs.

In all the ways here discussed the credit union management can exercise the functions of PLANNING, ORGANIZING, DIRECTING, COORDINATING, AND CONTROLLING. These functions, described one way or another, are the heart of any kind of management.

Credit Union Management's Educational Responsibilities

It has been said that education is the heart and soul of cooperation. Members of a cooperative must be able to make their own decisions, to elect their own officials expecting their choices to be wise ones, and to take responsibility for their own actions. All of these potentialities are absolutely necessary to the proper functioning of a credit union. The members must know a great deal about many areas of their lives, including economics, politics and community problems. They must be educated.

Too often education is taken to mean nothing more than formal schooling. If a man holds a school certificate, many people would say that he is automatically educated. But so far as cooperatives are concerned, education has a different meaning. When a cooperator speaks of education he means mastery of the skills which will enable a man to manage his own affairs.

If a man understands how to do his job well and what responsibility means; if he understands enough about life to make his own decisions about the things that affect him most closely; and if he has enough honest, realistic confidence in his own ability to do his job and to take responsibility for his decisions, he is educated enough to be a working, participating member of a cooperative. Many persons who have been all the way through a university still lack this kind of education.

Because of the importance of education to the running of a cooperative, credit union management has one more responsibility than the management of a profit company in the same field of finance: that of educating as many people as possible, members and non-members, in the ways of solving their own financial problems.

Credit unions cannot launch enormous propaganda campaigns, buying newspaper space and television and radio time, to convince people that joining a credit union is a panacea for their money problems.

For one thing, most credit unions cannot afford huge, spectacular publicity campaigns. For another, credit union principles discourage attempts to attract an enormous, bewildered membership who have no idea of how a credit union works. A credit union cannot afford to have a membership composed of those who are simply seeking a high-dividend investment or who would expect the credit union to handle all their financial matters for them. Credit unions have a duty to their country, themselves, and the entire cooperative movement to educate everyone they can as thoroughly as they can.

Because of this responsibility for education practically every credit union has an educational committee, made up of three or four members, as are the other committees. In most places, even where the supervisory and credit committees are elected separately by direct vote of the membership, the educational committee is usually appointed by the board of directors. Sometimes, the educational committee is placed under the direction of the vice-president, although there is no universal rule in the movement governing either the establishment or the direction of the educational committee.

The members of the educational committee may or may not be members of the board. It is better to find talented members who are not on any other committee and assign them to the educational committee, thus making wider use of the human resources.

Although the educational committee is not on the same administrative level as the supervisory committee and the credit committee, it should still be considered as a team of great importance. The board must be careful to see that the educational committee consists of persons with creative ability and the keen enthusiasm and willingness to work that inspires others.

The function of the educational committee is not only to educate the membership in the total program, but also to keep management informed of the response from members and potential members of the credit union.

For the first purpose the means available are limited only by the imagination of the educational committee. Leaflets on local interest rates, giving an honest comparison between the cost of credit-union loans and that of the loans of other agencies; lectures and films open to the public for little or no admission fee; regular newsletters that enable members to keep their legislators briefed on the credit union's operations and local problems—all these and other means are available to make sure that as many people as possible understand what is going on around them, as it applies to the credit union and the community at large.

For the purpose of maintaining contact within the organization a regular newsletter is ideal. Whether it consists of a few mimeographed pages stapled together or whether it is an impressive magazine with colored pictures does not matter as much as regular, not intermittent, publication once a month, or bimonthly, or quarterly, whatever the period.

Regularity is important. The members must learn to expect the newsletter at a certain time and look forward to it. If it gives an honest account of the credit union's activities over the period it covers, as well as information on important matters of economic or governmental or social interest outside the credit union, the newsletter will become an important arm of the educational program.

The educational committee can attract new members to the credit union by giving people the facts they need on a host of economic and financial subjects, so that they can see for themselves just how a credit union can be of use to them, and so that the people who do join will have no illusions.

In this connection the educational committee can help management to see to it that the credit union's operations are such that people will want to join when they do have all of the facts.

And by keeping the members up to date on credit union principles, and the facts about how these principles can best be put into practice, the educational committee can make sure that the members have enough background to make the decisions needed to improve the basic policies of the credit union.

A credit union cannot function in an educational vacuum. In a community where no one understands the nature or concepts of a cooperative it is important that the credit union be prepared to supply education. A credit union functions best when its members know what it is doing. This is one phase of education that should not be overlooked. For these reasons, credit union management relies on the educational committee to add one more function to the traditional "P.O.D.C.C." of all management—education, the essential factor in all cooperative endeavors.

V

Responsibilities and Qualities
of Credit Union Officers

This chapter will discuss in detail the responsibilities of credit union officers, what their work consists of, and what kind of person is needed to fill each position.

President

The president is the political leader of the credit union. He is elected by the board of directors to be their chairman, and also to act as chairman at the credit union's annual meeting. In relations with the general public he is the spokesman for the credit union.

Although the president's job is not so precise and technical as the treasurer's, the president must be as capable a man in his own field as the treasurer is in the area of business management, and must have many of the same qualities.

The president must be a leader and an organizer. He must be able to get the members to work smoothly together so that their officials can run an efficient business and govern it as the members wish. The board of directors will be made up of individuals, of whom most have their own ideas on how things should be done and may not be very tolerant of anyone else's ideas. At the annual meeting the members will not invariably agree with each other. The president must be able to persuade the people at the meetings he presides over to reconcile their differences so that decisions satisfactory to most of the group can be reached.

The president must generate enthusiasm for the credit union, radiate belief in its ideals, and show his dedication by being a hard worker. He must inspire by his own example. Once again, we are speaking not of talking enthusiasm but of working enthusiasm.

Since the president is the presiding officer, chairman of every board meeting and of the annual meeting, he must know how to conduct both small and large meetings in a relaxed, friendly way, so as to encourage participation and discussion and avoid confusion and bad feelings.

A knowledge of *Robert's Rules of Order,* the guide to formal parliamentary procedure, may be helpful for smoothing out arguments as to the order of business and complicated procedural situations. Generally, though, a meeting will run more smoothly if the procedure is kept as informal as possible, with no need to follow the strict complicated pattern set down by Robert's rules.

The president's day-to-day duties consist mainly of keeping the entire credit union running smoothly, through the other elected officials. He must be diplomatic—able to offer criticism in such a way that it is accepted without hurting anyone's feelings. He must be ready with advice and encouragement to members who seem to be having difficulties with their work and are beginning to lose heart. And occasionally, if the situation requires it, the president must be able to persuade a member who is really failing in his job to resign voluntarily and to bring about his replacement without ill-feeling.

In all of his dealings, both with the board and committees and with the total membership, the president must be dignified but not pompous, firm but never dictatorial. As the highest elected official of a democratic organization he has the opportunity of leading his fellow members to cooperative achievements they otherwise may never attain.

Vice-President

As his title suggests the vice-president is the executive official who stands ready to take over from the president if at any time the president is unable to perform his duties. The vice-president is often placed in charge of the educational committee, but his chief job is as a potential president.

By the very nature of the job the office of vice-president requires an unusual kind of man with very special qualities. The vice-president must be a quiet leader, who must be willing to take on responsibilities practically equal to the president's but still remain in the background, allowing the president to be the man whom the members see and hear from the most often.

The vice-president may be fully as qualified for leadership as the president. He must have many of the same abilities for bringing people together and bringing about a settlement of differences. He must have the same enthusiasm for his work. Many vice-presidents eventually move on to the presidency because they do have the qualities needed for the presidency and because their experience as vice-presidents further qualifies them for the job.

While he holds his office, however, the vice-president must give support to the man who is already president.

Secretary

The secretary has the important job of keeping accurate minutes of the meetings of the board of directors and the general membership. Most of the official correspondence from the board of directors to members or to others outside of the credit union is prepared by the secretary unless the board directs others to do this. In discharging these responsibilities the secretary enables the credit union to follow a consistent course of action and to express its policies clearly in its official correspondence.

In many credit unions the treasurer is permitted by law to hold the position of secretary. Usually this is the only dual-officer position permitted in credit unions.

Treasurer

The treasurer has the heaviest daily duties of all officials. In most credit unions, except those large enough to have a paid staff, the treasurer is the general manager. At the same time, until the credit union can afford to hire employees, he is the bookkeeper and often the secretary. For these reasons the treasurer may be paid. Usually he is the only elected official who is permitted by law to accept a salary or even an honorarium.

As general manager the treasurer is the man who has the most contact of all with other members. He is in charge of all the money the credit union accepts or disburses. When members come in to deposit or withdraw their money the treasurer either accepts the money from them or gives them a check for the money they have withdrawn.

The treasurer is in charge of collection of all loans. He must either collect the loans himself or supervise other directors or employees designated to collect loans.

When a member or a potential member comes to the credit union for advice on financial problems or for information, the treasurer is the one who usually acts as a counsellor or information officer, whichever he is called on to be.

At the same time, the treasurer must safeguard the books and records. He must do all of the bookkeeping or supervise others who do it. He is directly accountable for all of the money the credit union possesses. All financial statements usually are prepared and signed by the treasurer. He is, in short, responsible for all of the money in the credit union and the bookwork involved in accounting for the money, and for reporting the financial condition of the credit union.

Qualifications for Treasurer

In electing a treasurer, the members must take into consideration the amount of work the office of treasurer involves, as well as the qualifications requisite for the position. If the treasurer is the only officer who may be paid for his official duties, it is all the more important to fill the position with the right person.

Although a great deal of the treasurer's work involves bookkeeping, bookkeeping ability is nowhere near the most important quality to look for in a treasurer. Of course, the treasurer will eventually have to learn bookkeeping, as it is an essential part of his job. Most people can learn bookkeeping in a relatively short time. Some are more adept than others, but generally a treasurer can pick up bookkeeping in a few months if he works steadily to learn it.

The more important qualifications and skills a treasurer must have are not so easily acquired. They apply in some degree to all the other officers.

Ability to get along with people

The knack of getting along with people is highly important, as the treasurer's job brings him into contact with so many in the course of a day's work. There are several qualities which make getting along with people much easier.

Need for patience

To get along with the people he has to work with a treasurer must have patience. People are unreasonable in many different ways, and dealing with them may not be the most pleasant job in the world.

The treasurer is the man to whom the members bring their complaints about the credit union's operations. The treasurer may rightly feel that many of these complaints are unfair and unjustified, but he is still obliged to listen patiently and do what he can to ensure that he and the complaining member understand each other. He must remain courteous, as difficult as this may be if he is being harassed unjustifiably.

Because he has to collect payments on loans, the treasurer has to face many trying situations. Certain members will be reluctant to pay what they owe. Others will disappear when their loan payment comes due. Some will tell the treasurer that they "just can't pay." The treasurer's job is to convince the reluctant, to find the ones who have disappeared, and to sit down with those who say they cannot pay and try to figure out with them just why they cannot and how they can manage to do it as soon as possible. All of this work takes an enormous amount of patience.

The daily frustrations of a treasurer's work may exhaust the patience of an ordinary person at the end of a single day. But a credit union treasurer must have enough patience to take the difficulties in stride week after week and still remain pleasant. Even people who think they would like to become members will take the treasurer's conduct into consideration when deciding whether or not to join the credit union.

Understanding people

To get along with people a man must understand them. Profit-making businesses know this understanding builds profits. Credit unions consider it even more important because understanding is essential to democratic participation. A credit union treasurer cannot do his job well without understanding the members for whom he works and the other officials with whom he serves in management.

In the course of his work the treasurer must be able to advise people on their problems—and not only on financial problems. Often a man will be in debt because of some personal problem. His wife may be sick. He may have an aged relative for whom he is responsible. Or his son may have run into trouble with the police, for which he may have to pay a heavy fine.

In counselling people about loans, one of the treasurer's greatest responsibilities, he must show that he genuinely understands the problem, that he understands how deeply the member feels about it, and that he is concerned to help solve the problem, either through the credit union or some other means.

It is not enough for the treasurer to be only a listener to sad stories or, for that matter, to be a sharer of good news. He is the symbol of the entire credit union to the member who comes to him for help or for congratulation. He is expected to mobilize the support of the group in sharing the problems and happiness of each member.

Sensitiveness toward the people with whom he is working, their feelings, and the real problems that may confront them help a treasurer to understand their weaknesses and the devices they may use to hide the real problems they are ashamed of; and this sensitiveness may bring lasting feelings of goodwill from those whose only need was a pat on the back at the right moment.

Ability to keep confidence

Closely connected with the quality of understanding is the ability to keep a confidence. This ability is all-important to a treasurer's work.

There have been cases where credit union members have told their treasurer what they would not tell anyone else. Trouble with the law, alcoholism, disease, and illegitimacy are still problems which plague too many families. In the course of his work a treasurer is bound to run across members with problems which must be kept in absolute confidence.

If a man confides in the treasurer for help on such a matter the treasurer must keep the information strictly and completely to himself. It does not matter if "everyone else in town" knows already. It is still important that "everyone" did not find out from the credit union's treasurer.

It goes without saying that confidence should not be betrayed. But a treasurer must be able to keep an especially tight hold on his tongue. A credit union should elect no one treasurer who cannot keep confidences, no matter how good his bookkeeping may be.

Must like people

Finally, in order to get along with people, the treasurer must really like them and enjoy working with them. This quality underlies the others. A person who likes people and has these other qualities will find them willing to confide in him. Members usually think of their personal contact with the treasurer as representative of the entire credit union. If these contacts are warm and friendly they build membership participation and support. If not, even a dedicated, hard-working treasurer will never enjoy the personal satisfactions that are perhaps the best compensation he will receive.

Importance of honesty

Need it be emphasized that the treasurer must be an unswervingly honest man? He must know the difference between his own money and the money entrusted to him by the credit union. Because the treasurer handles all of the credit union's money and all of its books and records, a dishonest treasurer can seriously damage a credit union in a very short time, or even cause its ruin.

In consequence, the members must make sure that they elect a treasurer whose honesty is deep and strong enough to resist the temptations to which he is exposed when he handles money—more money than he has ever seen before.

Generally, people know which members of their own group are honest and which are either dishonest or weak in character, and can elect their officials accordingly. Most members find it easy to remember that the honesty of their treasurer is the main measure of the security of their savings.

Enthusiasm

A treasurer must be enthusiastic about his work. He must radiate enthusiasm so that the other members are encouraged by his example.

This does not mean that the treasurer is to be a man with a loud voice and a flag and a lot of leaflets who is always going around lecturing the other members with platitudes. It means that the treasurer must be quietly and sincerely dedicated to his work and must show that he takes his job seriously and contributes his best to it.

A treasurer's enthusiasm must show itself in his willingness to help others who need help, oftentimes without being asked. It must show in his ability to come up with a smile or a friendly remark for a visitor after a hard day of difficult bookkeeping or loan collections. It must show itself in the treasurer's willingness to take on difficult jobs and see them through, jobs such as traveling miles into the back country actually to take the credit union to members who cannot come to the treasurer's office—if he has one—or such as staying at the office and working at the books until they balance, even though it may involve using up a lot of lamp-fuel and insect repellent.

Enthusiasm of this kind is contagious. If the treasurer is enthusiastic the other members of the credit union are likely to get the same enthusiasm and apply it to their own activities in the credit union and the community.

Ability to keep goals in sight

The treasurer, as the general manager, must be able to remember the goals and principles of the credit union and keep them constantly in mind. He must be able to look up from his books and his everyday problems once in awhile and ask himself: "Is this credit union on the right track? Are we encouraging our members to save, as we're supposed to? Is our loan service within reach of as many people as possible? Are our plans such that we'll be able to stay in close touch with all of our members as we expand, or are we turning into just one more big savings-and-loan company? And, most important of all, are the members really in control or is management taking over?"

Very often the treasurer will have so many things on his mind that he will not have time to look at the overall picture of how the credit union is running and where it is going. He must therefore make it a part of his everyday job to keep the goals within sight, particularly to make sure that the credit union functions as a democratic cooperative organization.

Willingness to learn

No matter how well educated or how well principled he may be, the treasurer can always learn from others how to do a better job. He will find help in books, pamphlets, and magazines; and in discussions with others who also are willing to learn, not only in the credit union movement, but also in the fields of management, cooperatives, and world affairs.

Finding Right Officers

Credit union members must remember that no one is perfect and that they probably never will find officials who before they take office have all of the qualities listed here. Many of these skills and personal characteristics must be acquired through working experience.

However, a group who have worked together for a while generally know who among their own number is honest, hardworking, cheerful, good-natured, and reliable, and they will be able to elect representatives who have or who will develop these characteristics.

Persons who have never worked with voluntary organizations are often surprised to find how many good leaders will work without remuneration. Since ability on the job is commonly associated with the amount of salary a man receives, people often assume that money is the only attraction for able workers. Credit unions demonstrate how wrong this assumption can be; in fact, the very opposite is true.

Able workers are obviously attracted by high salaries, but so are those who are mediocre or even incompetent. On the other hand, who else except the unusual man or woman is willing to work in a common cause without payment? By offering satisfactions far beyond the usual honoraria, credit unions get unusually dedicated leaders. And they get them from every occupation and profession.

VI

Leagues, CUNA International
and Their Affiliates

Cooperation among Cooperatives

One of the basic principles the credit union movement has maintained throughout its existence is the belief in cooperation and mutual support among credit unions, just as the belief in cooperation among individual citizens for the common good has been important to the movement. Credit unions believe in lending some of their individual strength to the common effort with other credit unions, for purposes of improved educational facilities, greater capacity for spreading cooperative and credit union ideals, and the strength and mutual protection that unity breeds.

In practical terms this means that most credit unions, in any country, find that they must eventually form themselves into a federation of some kind. Founders of the credit union movement such as William Raiffeisen in Germany, Alphonse DesJardins in Canada, and Edward A. Filene and Roy Bergengren in the United States realized that, for the credit unions to survive the tremendous odds against them, they would have to unite for common protection. And because of their willingness to unify, credit unions have managed to survive and prosper with little reliance, if any, on any benevolent outside source, government or otherwise.

In Raiffeisen's time a credit union was not formed until its members agreed that it would join the existing federation. This compulsion no longer exists in most countries, but the majority of credit unions still feel some obligation to join the closest available league or federation.

In many cases credit unions owe their formation to a volunteer representing some league or federation of credit unions. If a credit union exists only because someone representing a league took the time to help organize it, educating leaders and gaining the interest of potential members, that credit union will naturally feel some obligation to join the league that helped make its existence possible.

So, because credit unions are cooperatives, and dedicated to the cooperative ideal whose principles include cooperation between credit unions, leagues or federations of credit unions usually start to form as soon as individual credit unions are organized.

Structure of Credit Union Movement

The actual structure of a credit union movement may take many different forms. There is no set pattern which a country must follow in setting up its credit union movement. Rather, it is important that credit union members design their movement along the pattern that best suits their own needs.

In the United States and Canada individual credit unions have combined to form state or provincial credit union leagues, which in turn belong to CUNA International, Inc. Although this pattern does not have to be applied to the credit union movement of any other country, it serves as an example of how a credit union movement can be established.

Credit Union Leagues and Federations

Credit-union leagues and federations are nonprofit, voluntary organizations of credit unions, supported by the dues of their member credit unions. Their aim is service, as is the aim of the credit unions themselves.

Federations and leagues are formed on a geographic basis. There is a credit union league for almost every state of the United States, and almost every province of Canada.

In addition, some of the smaller countries or territories where credit unions have been established have their own credit union leagues, which are organized along the same lines as the state and provincial leagues.

Credit union leagues are organized to provide service to their member credit unions. The leagues give the credit unions which belong to them protection, assistance, information, and a source of materials and supplies necessary to everyday credit union operations.

Protection

In the way of protection, the state or provincial league works to obtain and maintain legislation favorable to credit unions in their area.

In many places banks and loan companies fear credit union competition, and seek to pressure legislators into passing laws which would make credit union operation difficult, if not impossible. Since credit unions' opponents often control a great deal of money and are comparatively well-organized among themselves, individual credit unions are helpless to block their efforts.

A credit union league, however, presents a more formidable opponent to anti-credit-union legislation. The leagues, because they represent large numbers of potential voters, are often able to influence legislatures greatly to be fair to credit unions.

Because leagues command a larger amount of money than could any individual credit union they are able to buy advertising space in newspapers, on radio, and on television, so that the public can know as much about credit unions as it knows about banks and other loan institutions. In this way also credit union leagues give credit unions a fighting chance in a competitive system. Internal protection from dishonesty is also important to credit unions. Leagues provide, through .CUNA International, a strong fidelity bond program; and some leagues have an auditing service on a fee basis.

Other Types of Service

Credit union leagues provide valuable assistance to their member credit unions in many ways, starting with advice and guidance in the first plans to organize and continuing through every phase of their operation to liquidation if that becomes necessary.

Skilled advisers are available in the league office or they travel to individual credit unions which request their services, to help the credit union find out just what its problems are and what can be done to solve them.

Also, credit union leagues sponsor conventions and conferences at which representatives of member credit unions meet to discuss common problems, so that solutions achieved by some credit unions will be made available to all of the league's member credit unions. This type of assistance also provides social contacts for credit union leaders which help to strengthen the sense of solidarity that comes with league membership.

Leagues provide their credit unions with the latest news and information on current events in the areas of most interest —legislation, world extension, technical advances and similar topics. Credit union leagues alone or through CUNA International carry on studies of credit union operations, and publish the results for the benefit for their members.

Many credit union personnel receive special training made available by their league to enable them to perform their jobs most effectively. Through courses and seminars, credit union leagues educate officials and employees in new methods of credit union operation, to help them serve their credit union better.

In addition, credit union leagues provide a contact between the members of an individual credit union and the international organization of credit unions, CUNA International, Incorporated, whose board of directors are elected by state and provincial credit union leagues.

Member credit unions often look to their leagues as a source of insurance; also bookkeeping materials, printed publicity matter, and other supplies necessary to the running of a credit union. The ways in which the credit union movement does these things will be explained later in this chapter.

Help Organize New Credit Unions

One of the most important functions of a credit union league is to help organize new credit unions in the area it serves.

Credit union leagues often have trained advisers at their disposal—sometimes paid staff, sometimes unpaid volunteers —who visit groups requesting their services. League organization workers help the group to work out the solutions of pre-organizational problems, set up the machinery for electing credit union officers and handling funds, and fill out the application for a charter.

Often the league will send a recommendation to the supervisory agency of the region, advising the agency to grant registration to a group whom a league organizer has been helping. If the league has been doing a good job, the government officer in charge will come to respect league recommendations, and may look to the league for advice on credit union operations in his jurisdiction.

In some places credit union leagues have a provision in their bylaws which allows any new credit union in the region automatically to become a member of the league for a trial period of sixty days, during which time the new credit union may receive most of the benefits of full league membership. At the end of the trial period the new credit union may decide for itself whether it wants to make formal application for membership in the league.

By providing a source of advice and protection to new credit unions, a credit union league can do a great deal to promote the growth of credit unions in the area it represents.

In all the ways mentioned above credit union leagues provide service to their member credit unions, service which is highly essential to healthy credit union growth and operation, but which the member credit unions would find it difficult or impossible to provide for themselves.

Design of State or Provincial Credit Union League

As nations have found that representative government is an ideal method of governing a large number of people according to the people's own wishes, so has the credit union movement adopted the system of representative democracy to govern its different divisions.

In Chapter IV we noted that each individual credit union is governed by men and women elected by the members to carry on the day-to-day business of the credit union. In the structure of a credit union league the organization is governed by people elected not directly by the credit union members themselves but by representatives of the members who are elected by the vote of the members.

In a league which numbers two or three hundred credit unions among its members, involving over a hundred thousand credit union members, this representative system allows the league to be governed efficiently and, at the same time, provides the members of its credit unions with a direct line of contact with the governing body of the league. Let us see how this system works in a particular league.

Chapter

For the purpose of bringing representation to the members, the credit union league divides itself into sections called chapters. The chapters are defined by the governing body of the league partly on a geographic basis and partly on the number of credit unions and members in the area.

A group of at least twenty credit unions with a combined membership of not less than five hundred people may apply to the league for registration as a chapter. Each chapter consists of the credit unions in a specific area which are members of the league. Credit unions which are not members of the league may not belong to any chapter of the league, and a credit union may not belong to a chapter in any area of the state or province other than its own area.

Each chapter is governed by a board of representatives. Each member credit union is entitled to elect two representatives, who are chosen from among the management of their own credit union by the vote of the members of the credit union.

The board of representatives then elects its own set of officers and, most importantly, either one or two representatives to the board of directors of the league.

These representatives are known as league directors. Chapters having between twenty and fifty member credit unions are entitled to elect one league director each. Chapters having more than fifty member credit unions are entitled to elect two league directors.

A chapter with more than fifty member credit unions may apply to the league board of directors to allow it to divide into two separate chapters, provided that each chapter has at least twenty member credit unions. When a chapter numbers more than one hundred twenty credit unions among its members the bylaws require that the league board of directors divide it into two chapters.

Many of the league's activities are carried on at the chapter level. Primary purposes of the chapter, aside from electing league directors, include sponsoring educational programs such as training sessions for officers, assistance in organizing new credit unions, and promotional and public-relations projects. The chapter serves as the working agency of the league in its own specific geographical area, utilizing volunteers to multiply the effectiveness of the paid league workers.

League Board of Directors

The league directors elected by the chapter boards of representatives throughout the state or province together form the league board of directors, whose job it is to manage the league. League directors serve for two-year terms and meet regularly four times a year. The bylaws of the league require that league directors report in writing to their chapters on the proceedings of all such meetings.

The league board of directors elects from its own number an executive committee consisting of a president, vice-president, secretary, and treasurer, as is the case with the individual credit unions. The duties of these officials differ slightly from those of the officials having the same titles on the credit-union level; the league treasurer does not serve in as much of a managing-directorship capacity as does the treasurer of a credit union, but the duties of the president, vice-president, and secretary are similar to those of their credit union counterparts.

The league board of directors hires a managing director to act as an assistant secretary and as an assistant treasurer at meetings. In actual practice the managing director is the top executive official in the league. He signs all checks and contracts made by the league and takes charge of most of the league business on a day-to-day basis. It is the managing director's work which corresponds most closely to the duties of a credit union treasurer.

The managing director may hold a position on the league board by virtue of his job. All the same, the managing director is an employee of the league and must follow the directives of the rest of the league board of directors, who have the authority to dismiss or retain a managing director.

In addition to the quarterly board meetings the league also holds one regular membership meeting every year, attended by two delegates from each member credit union. At this meeting, the credit union representatives, elected by the members of their own credit unions, have the power to review any action taken by the league board of directors, and possibly to reverse some board decisions, provided that such reversal does not result in the breach of any contract made by the league board.

This meeting corresponds to the annual membership meeting of the credit union. The decisions of the representatives attending this annual league-membership meeting represent the ultimate authority in the credit union league, thus bringing the real authority in the league back to representatives directly responsible to the members of the credit unions.

The credit union league, once again, is basically a democratic organization bound by the same principles which govern the management of each individual credit union. It is important that league office-holders, both on the chapter level and on the league level, remember that they are ultimately responsible to the individual credit union members.

CUNA—Credit Union National Association, Incorporated

In 1934 the Credit Union National Association was organized with the help of Edward A. Filene, the patron of the credit union movement in the United States. The Credit Union National Association, usually abbreviated CUNA, was designed to serve as the national organization for United States credit unions, performing the same services for credit union leagues that the leagues performed for their credit unions. CUNA's members were to be credit union leagues, although individual credit unions have been permitted to join CUNA in areas where no league existed.

In 1940 CUNA amended its bylaws to allow credit union leagues throughout the Western Hemisphere to join. Among the first credit union leagues to join CUNA from outside the United States were the provincial leagues of Canada. Later, in a historic meeting in 1954, the CUNA board of directors voted to establish a world-extension department, and through it to assist the peoples of other countries in establishing credit unions for themselves. Thus CUNA became an international organization of credit union leagues while still serving as the national organization for the credit union movement of the United States.

In 1958 CUNA again amended its bylaws to extend its field of membership to leagues all over the world. At year-end 1964 membership in the organization had grown to include 77 credit union leagues of credit unions in some 70 countries.

CUNA Becomes CUNA International

As the new nations came into their own after World War II, and their leagues affiliated with CUNA after 1958, a dilemma arose: how to give national and regional movements a place to decide matters essentially of first importance to themselves while retaining the international organization for worldwide policy making.

At the present time, the overwhelming majority of the world's affiliated credit unions are located in either the United States and its territories or Canada. Credit unions in all of the other countries of the world combined account for a minority of the credit unions represented either directly or through leagues in the world organization. The reasons for this disparity do not lie in any fault of the credit union movements outside of the North America; rather they lie in the size of the populations of the countries of North America, and in the industrial and agricultural development of these countries.

Not only do United States and Canadian credit unions account for the majority of the membership of the world credit union movement. They also account for most of the movement's funds. The fact is that no international credit union organization could function effectively today without the financial resources of the United States and Canadian credit union movements. United States and Canadian credit unions are wealthy largely because their countries are wealthy, and they have used their financial strength to help credit unions gets started in other countries. These credit union movements in the other countries are still comparatively small, but their combined voting strength in CUNA is becoming significant. Many credit union people in the United States became fearful that, as CUNA's world membership increased, they might find themselves outvoted on essentially national issues by the leagues of other countries. To a lesser extent they questioned the financial burden that might be imposed on them by this voting.

NATIONAL FORUM PLAN

In 1964 the CUNA board of directors changed the name of the organization to CUNA International, Incorporated, and also instituted a new method of conducting business, which they called the forum plan.

Before the forum plan was introduced all CUNA directors voted on all CUNA business, even business which concerned only the credit unions of one country. There was no machinery to allow national credit union movements to handle their own affairs. The United States had no national credit union organization outside CUNA, and many American representatives felt that there should be some way that they could debate and conduct their own country's credit union business without bringing everything they discussed to a vote of the entire organization.

For a time, some members of CUNA wanted to set up a separate national credit union organization for the United States alone. Others felt that, since CUNA as an organization was still forced to rely so heavily upon United States credit unions, the international organization might suffer if these credit unions formed another organization for themselves.

To avoid splitting up the international organization while allowing a measure of self-rule to national credit union movements, CUNA, when it became CUNA International, Inc., instituted a plan whereby the representatives of each nation meet in national forums to consider their own country's credit union business immediately prior to every meeting of the CUNA International board of directors.

The national forums report to the entire international board of directors their decisions on any resolutions or proposals which come up at their meetings. The international board of directors may debate or discuss these proposals but the directors from the nation concerned have the final vote on the proposals in their respective forums, with no other directors voting.

The forum plan is designed to allow countries to determine for themselves the affairs which affect them alone. It is also designed to maintain close contact among credit union leagues of different countries and to allow credit unions of each country to use the international board of directors as a sounding board for their ideas.

The national forum plan has made no change in the actual structure of CUNA International, Inc. The same representatives sit on both their own national forums and the CUNA International board of directors.

Structure of CUNA International, Inc.

Like the credit union leagues which make up the majority of its membership, CUNA International is a non-profit organization, supported by the dues of its member credit union leagues and governed by representatives of those leagues.

For purposes of representation and administration the leagues comprising CUNA International, Inc., are divided into twelve districts. Eleven of these districts are on the North American continent (including the island of Puerto Rico) and the twelfth covers all the rest of the world.

The board of directors is elected by the member leagues. Each league is entitled to elect from one to five directors, depending on the number of members of credit unions in the league. At its annual meetings the board of directors, now numbering 250, elects from its own number an executive committee to run the organization between board meetings. The executive committee of CUNA International consists of a president, one vice-president from each of the 12 districts, a secretary, and a treasurer.

One of the important duties of the executive committee is to hire a managing director to run the various departments through which the organization extends services to its members from its headquarters in Filene House at Madison, Wisconsin, U. S. A., and offices in other countries.

Services Provided by CUNA International and Its Affiliates

CUNA International and its affiliated organizations provide services to member leagues in much the same way that the leagues serve their member credit unions, working through specialized departmental staff. *Promote, perfect, protect—* every service is designed to accomplish these purposes. A listing of the various CUNA departments will illustrate the range of help available to leagues, credit unions and credit union members, in achieving these avowed objectives of the international credit union movement:

1. To spread the understanding of credit union principles throughout the world, to create an atmosphere of acceptance of these principles, and to foster the organization of credit unions through which these principles can be put to work.

2. To promote the organization of credit union leagues, associations and other agencies whose function it is to serve credit unions and the credit union movement.

3. To encourage thrift, wise use of credit, and prudent management of personal and family resources.

4. To encourage participation in the democratic processes of credit union control at all levels, and in the exercise of officer responsibility.

5. To offer information and guidance to credit union board members, officers, and committee members to the end that the credit unions they represent will offer a maximum of thrift and credit service of the highest quality, service consistent with the ideals of the credit union movement in harmony with the basic policies herein expressed.

6. To establish and maintain good working relationships with chartering and supervising agencies of credit unions, with the intent to facilitate the work of such agencies, to reduce liquidations to a minimum, and to

assure freedom of action on the part of credit unions in the performance of their work.

7. To foster legislation helpful to the achievement of credit union purposes, and to combat legislation hostile to these purposes.

DEPARTMENTS OF CUNA INTERNATIONAL, INC.

Advertising and Promotion
Canadian Office
Conference Coordinator
CUES (Credit Union Executive Services) Coordinator
Education
Electronic Data Processing
League Management Consultant
Legislative
Insurance Services
Organization-Expansion
Personnel
Publications
Washington Office
World Extension
Public Relations
Research and Economics
Defense (Army, Navy, Air Force) Credit Union Council
Comptroller

CUNA SUPPLY COOPERATIVE

The CUNA Supply Cooperative is also a non-profit and member-owned organization, its members being CUNA International's member leagues. Each member organization sends one delegate to cast one vote at the annual membership meeting, and twelve of these delegates, one each from each CUNA district, are elected as CUNA Supply directors for three-year terms. These directors in turn elect an executive committee which employs a managing director. Traditionally, the same managing director serves both CUNA International and CUNA Supply Cooperative. All CUNA supply directors must also be directors of CUNA International.

CUNA Supply Cooperative was organized in 1936 to provide a source of credit union supplies and equipment for credit unions and their organizations. Specialization in this field enables CUNA Supply to manufacture or procure through other suppliers the most advanced types of bookkeeping stationery and promotional and advertising materials available. Annual volume in 1964 exceeded one and a quarter million dollars.

Insurance Affiliates

SIMILARITIES BETWEEN CREDIT UNIONS AND INSURANCE COOPERATIVES

As we shall see in this chapter, credit unions have been extremely successful in extending their activities to the field of insurance. It might be noted that there are similarities between credit unions and insurance cooperatives that make it logical for them to operate side-by-side.

Credit unions provide their members with protection from disasters, and with the means to enjoy a better life, by assuring them of financial help when they need it most. They know from experience that ordinarily not all of the members will want loans, or the return of their share investments, at the same time. Their members' pooled savings provide an adequate reserve for the kind of help they expect. And the integrity of their members in repaying loans promptly, together with good management, enables them to pay minimum interest charges for their loans while receiving maximum dividends on their savings.

Insurance cooperatives provide protection and peace of mind to people or organizations that want to be protected against losses of various kinds, by guaranteeing to pay all or a part of these losses. To pay these amounts the insurance cooperative must build up reserves from payments made by those wanting to be insured. These payments are called premiums. Thus, insurance is a pooling of reserves that have been built up from premium payments to take care of future losses.

The amount of reserves needed depends on the type of insurance to be provided and the conditions that affect the particular risk to be insured. In the field of life insurance a great deal of experience has been acquired, and a monumental body of statistics has been accumulated, which enables statisticians to forecast accurately the amount of reserves needed to insure the lives of people in the amounts desired. In the fields of casualty and fire insurance the experiences of the past and the statistics also help to provide some idea of the average losses that may be expected on the various types of risks to be insured. Since these losses are not so predictable the risks are spread among the insurance companies by various means so that all the insured losses in a particular disaster —such as a calamitous fire—do not fall on any one company.

In cooperative insurance companies the people or organizations that pay the premiums are the owners of the company and they share in the total costs of providing the service. Their integrity in helping the insurance company to avoid losses and their ability to provide efficient management result in their paying minimum premiums for their protection.

CUNA Mutual Insurance Society and CUMIS Insurance Society

Credit unions have found that cooperation pays in many ways. In addition to their leagues, CUNA International and CUNA Supply Cooperative, credit unions and their members own several insurance companies in the United States. Foremost among these is CUNA Mutual Insurance Society, founded in 1935 with the help of Edward A. Filene, now providing various forms of life insurance to credit unions for their members—and directly to credit union members—in a growing number of countries. CUNA Mutual insures thousands of credit unions and its policy coverage runs into the billions of dollars today, but its beginnings were as humble as those of the credit unions.

In 1935 in the state of Wisconsin, where some of the first credit unions in the United States were organized, a lineman working for an electric company borrowed $250 from his credit union; two of his friends signed the loan contract as his co-makers. A few weeks later the lineman was killed in an accident while repairing a high-tension line. Although the co-makers repaid the loan as they had promised, the credit union decided that something should be done in the future so that a member's debts would not become a burden on his friends or his family in the event of his death. CUNA leaders were consulted and, with the help of Edward A. Filene, a small sum of money was collected to form the CUNA Mutual Insurance Society.

They found a ready reception because CUNA leaders were becoming disturbed about the practice already started among some credit unions of selling commercial life-insurance policies to their borrowers at what amounted to a profit for the credit union.

The new insurance society started out by offering a very simple type of life insurance but one which very few of the established life-insurance companies had offered up to that time: loan protection (or borrowers') insurance. The plan was that the credit union would agree to pay the insurance society enough premium to provide life insurance on all of its borrowers; the society would agree to pay off the balance of any outstanding loan if the borrower died before the loan was paid in full. This was group insurance, although individual policies were also written. The purpose of this insurance was simply "The debt shall die with the debtor."

CUNA Mutual was successful with this new insurance almost from the start and a few years later inaugurated another life-insurance service for the members of credit unions. This was called life-savings insurance. It was also a form of group insurance, enabling all the members in a credit union to purchase life insurance in amounts based on their individual savings, by having their credit union contract with the society for the entire group.

Thus credit unions took advantage of their strength as individual cooperatives and they pooled their purchasing power in the insurance field to provide new kinds of life insurance that satisfied the needs of their members. Loan-protection insurance has succeeded to a large extent in making credit union debts die with the debtors. And life-savings insurance is added proof to millions of credit union members that savings make sense.

The CUNA Mutual Insurance Society has now become a large cooperative corporation owned by those who hold its policies. CUNA Mutual policyholder-owners, known as *policy-*

owners, include both credit unions making use of group contracts and individual credit union members who can afford to buy insurance protection on their own.

CUNA Mutual is managed by a board of directors elected by and from its members, in this case the credit unions and members who are the policyowners. It is strictly a non-profit service organization, turning all profits back to the members in the form of dividends or improved service.

People in many parts of the world today are still burdened with the problems which led to the founding of CUNA Mutual Insurance Society. They cannot say that debts die with the debtor. Instead many families are still struggling to pay off loans and interest on loans incurred by their fathers or even their grandfathers. The injustice is obvious; people are forced to shoulder a load which was passed on to them without their consent. They may spend their lifetime burdened with these debts and interest that accumulates to an amount greater than that of the original loan. And this is just as true in parts of the United States and other developed countries as it is in the newest of the developing countries. Or they face the danger of losing their homes or other property from fire, flood, or other disasters. Individually they cannot protect themselves. As a group with savings and experience in financial management they can protect themselves much better with cooperative insurance.

The CUMIS Insurance Society was organized in 1960 as an affiliate of and by CUNA Mutual to specialize in fire and casualty insurance. Common-stock purchases by credit union members and their organizations add to the original capital invested by CUNA Mutual. Here again is an example of what people can do for themselves in the related field of insurance after they have acquired the basic experience of managing their own money in credit unions.

League Life Insurance Company and Members' Mutual Insurance Company

Several of the United States leagues own and control insurance companies which stimulate competition for CUNA Mutual, as well as for the non-credit—union-owned insurance companies that do most of the business with credit unions.

The Michigan Credit Union League owns the League Life Insurance Company which now writes over $2 billion of loan-protection life savings and family-group life insurance for Michigan credit unions and their members. Family-group life insurance insures the breadwinner in the family with fixed amount and provides other members of his family with lesser amounts of life insurance to cover burial expenses. The member authorizes the credit union to pay the premiums out of his savings account, and all members benefit from the lower rates available to groups. Unlike the other credit union life-insurance policies, this insurance does not depend on the amount of the member's savings or his loan. It is simply another way for credit union members to pool their resources through their credit unions, their league, and their insurance company.

In Texas the league-owned Members' Mutual Insurance Company writes automobile insurance for members of credit unions which own the Texas Credit Union League. Individual credit union members could not cope with the problem, but they have had good experience in their own company. Automobile-insurance costs are mounting everywhere as drivers neglect their responsibilities for loss-prevention, and as companies seek higher profits for engaging in this risky business. Developing countries may take heed of the Texas experience and build their auto-insurance plans on the foundation of credit unions.

OTHER AFFILIATIONS OF CUNA INTERNATIONAL AND LEAGUES

CUNA International is a member of the Cooperative League of the U.S.A., which in turn is a member of the International Cooperative Alliance, and some individual leagues maintain the same affiliation. Similar memberships are held in the United States and, through it the International, Chamber of Commerce. Credit unions are now becoming more important both in the world of cooperatives and the world of business and the contacts they make in these organizations are important to an understanding of their unique place as people's banks, operated as businesses with a cooperative philosophy.

Structure of The Credit Union Movement

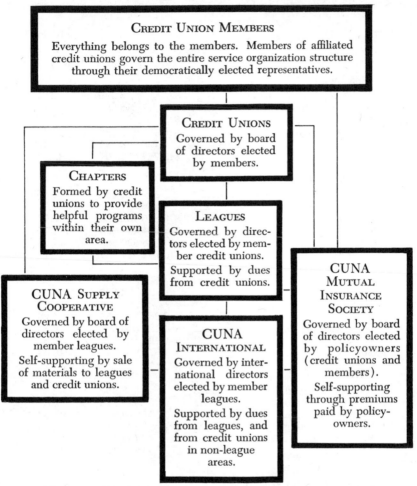

CREDIT UNION MEMBERS

Everything belongs to the members. Members of affiliated credit unions govern the entire service organization structure through their democratically elected representatives.

CREDIT UNIONS

Governed by board of directors elected by members.

CHAPTERS

Formed by credit unions to provide helpful programs within their own area.

LEAGUES

Governed by directors elected by member credit unions.

Supported by dues from credit unions.

CUNA MUTUAL INSURANCE SOCIETY

Governed by board of directors elected by policyowners (credit unions and members).

Self-supporting through premiums paid by policyowners.

CUNA SUPPLY COOPERATIVE

Governed by board of directors elected by member leagues.

Self-supporting by sale of materials to leagues and credit unions.

CUNA INTERNATIONAL

Governed by international directors elected by member leagues.

Supported by dues from leagues, and from credit unions in non-league areas.

CUNA International is an association of *leagues* of credit unions.

Leagues are voluntary, dues-supported associations of credit unions in any state, province, country, or other governmental unit having its own laws.

CUNA Mutual Insurance Society and CUNA Supply Cooperative are service organizations affiliated with CUNA International, the parent body.

Each credit union is a corporation chartered and supervised by a government agency. CUNA International is not a chartering agency.

The government agency which charters the credit union also assumes responsibility for its supervision. Credit unions welcome the supervision and protection afforded by the law.

SOURCE: International Credit Union Yearbook 1965 published by CUNA International, Inc.

The Worldwide Credit Union Movement in Summary

	END OF 1965	PERCENT OF GROWTH OVER 1964
WORLDWIDE		
Number of Credit Unions	45,970	2.91%
Number of Members	27,345,887	6.47
Savings	$12,167,523,317	13.76
Loans Outstanding	$10,407,156,087	16.75
Reserves	725,998,592	16.47
Total Assets	$13,722,095,407	13.72
UNITED STATES & TERRITORIES		
Number of Credit Unions	22,182	1.60%
Number of Members	16,655,609	6.64
Savings	$ 9,376,492,168	13.77
Loans Outstanding	$ 8,254,444,328	17.15
Reserves	$ 598,520,366	17.28
Total Assets	$10,644,547,524	13.71
CANADA		
Number of Credit Unions	4,645	0.83%
Number of Members	4,203,304	8.91
Savings	$ 2,282,910,053	14.28
Loans Outstanding	$ 1,720,898,861	16.83
Reserves	$ 120,612,829	12.64
Total Assets	$ 2,529,987,892	13.68
LATIN AMERICA*		
Number of Credit Unions	2,693	12.40%
Number of Members	558,711	5.83
Savings	$ 34,946,064	61.02
Loans Outstanding	$ 32,207,321	22.70
Reserves	$ 452,972	33.05
Total Assets	$ 39,569,742	42.93
ALL OTHER COUNTRIES†		
Number of Credit Unions	16,450	4.42%
Number of Members	5,928,263	4.41
Savings	$ 473,175,032	8.88
Loans Outstanding	$ 399,605,577	8.39
Reserves	$ 6,412,425	14.37
Total Assets	$ 507,990,249	12.21

*Includes estimates on unreported credit unions. More definite data will be provided by the CUNA-AID Program.

†India included, France not included.

By courtesy of CUNA International, Inc.

VII

Credit Union Bookkeeping
and the Financial Statement

Credit unions are a very simple form of business organization. They deal in only one commodity—money. And with few exceptions they deal only with their members. But like any other business organization they must keep records of their transactions and they use these records to produce reports that show the results of their business operations.

Bookkeeping records are maintained to show how much money has been received from members for entrance fees, shares, payments on loans and payments on interest; and how much money has been paid out to members for loans and withdrawals of shares; or paid out for operating expenses. With this information the treasurer can draw up a statement of income and expense that provides for each month and finally for the entire year the results—earnings or losses—from putting the members' money to work, and shows the sources of the income and the kinds of expense that brought about these results. Using the same information in another way, the treasurer prepares a balance sheet at the end of each month that shows the credit union's position in terms of what it owns and what it owes.

Most credit unions keep their bookkeeping records on a modified cash basis, that is, they record each transaction on their books as the cash is received or paid out. Thus it is relatively easy for the credit union to determine its earnings and its financial position at any given date.

This chapter is intended to help with an understanding of the basic bookkeeping system used by most credit unions, and thereby to explain the meaning of the credit-union financial statement.

Detailed bookkeeping instructions suitable for most credit unions, or adaptable to local practices, are available from CUNA Supply Co-operative, Box 333, Madison, Wisconsin 53701, U.S.A. The most comprehensive of these publications is the Accounting Manual for Federal Credit Unions (FCU 544) which is also available from the Government Printing Office, Washington, D.C. 20402, U.S.A.

PART I

Credit Union Bookkeeping

Let us start by reviewing briefly the theory on which the credit union bases its bookkeeping system. First, we recall that the credit union is a cooperative, doing business almost entirely with its members, but at the same time it is a business organization incorporated under a law which gives it legal status as a corporation *to own and to owe.* When members invest their money in shares of the credit union they exchange that money for certain legal rights in relation to the credit union. The credit union as a corporation *owes* them money for their shares. When they borrow money from the credit union, they are not borrowing their own money, they are borrowing money belonging to the corporation which has certain legal rights in relation to the member who has obtained a loan. The credit union *owns* the right to collect the loan.

Bookkeeping terminology uses the word "asset" *to describe something that is owned,* and the word "liability" *to describe something that is owed.* Members' shares, and reserves and earnings of the credit union that are being held for the members, are a special kind of liability which may be called "ownership" or "capital" but for our purposes in this chapter they will be referred to simply as liabilities.

Like other modern businesses the credit union uses the double-entry system of bookkeeping. Actually this system is centuries old, having its origins in ancient Rome and having been perfected by the Venetians of the 1400's. It is self-balancing and it minimizes errors or makes it easier to locate them when they do occur. Two entries are made for every transaction and two words are used to describe them, on the theory that every transaction involves a value received and a value given, that both these values are equal in amount and both must be recorded at the same time. These two entries are made on bookkeeping stationery that is divided into a column of figures on the left and a column of figures on the right.

These two words, which we shall encounter throughout the manuals and guidebooks on credit-union bookkeeping procedures, are—

> Debit—(from the Latin "he owes") to record acquisition of an *asset, or something that is owed to the credit union,* by a debtor. Debits are recorded on the left side of the bookkeeping form.

> Credit—(from the Latin "he entrusts") to record recognition of a *liability* or *something that the credit union owes* to a shareholder or other creditor. Credits are recorded on the right side of the bookkeeping form.

When the credit union receives money from a member or pays out money to a member it records changes in the asset and liability accounts by appropriate debits and credits. We could say in other words that it changes the amounts of what it owns and what it owes by appropriate notations on the lefthand side and on the righthand side of bookkeeping stationery. Let us take a few examples of typical transactions in a credit union using dollar currency, with shares valued at $5.00.

The credit union credits shares, giving a member's share account credit for $5.00 when he invests in one share; and debits the Cash-in-Bank account for money which the bank, where this money is deposited, owes to the credit union.

Entry No. 1.   Debit—Cash in Bank $5.00
              Credit—Shares $5.00

Or the credit union lends $500 to a member, recording by a debit to Loans that the member is in debt to the credit union on a $500.00 loan; and recording by a credit to Cash-in-Bank the reduction in the amount of money which the depository bank owes the credit union now that this money has been paid over to the borrowing member.

Entry No. 2.　Debit—Loans　　　$500.00
　　　　　　　 Credit—Cash in Bank　　$500.00

When the member withdraws $1.00 from his shares, the credit union pays him the cash out of its bank account; the credit union debits the member's share account to show that it owes him less money—it has reduced the liability for shares. At the same time the credit union owns less cash in the bank so it gives credit to that asset account.

Entry No. 3.　Debit—Shares　　　　$1.00
　　　　　　　 Credit—Cash in Bank　　$1.00

When the members pays back to the credit union $100.00 on his loan, the credit union gives him credit on his loan account for the payment and likewise debits the Cash-in-Bank account to show that the bank owes more money to the credit union for the amount deposited.

Entry No. 4.　Debit—Cash in Bank　$100.00
　　　　　　　 Credit—Loans　　　　　$100.00

Most of the credit union's bookkeeping is involved with share and loan transactions with its members. However, there is another activity which goes along at the same time and which requires more bookkeeping. The credit union puts its money to work mostly in loans to members but also in investments, and this results in earnings or income for the credit union from the interest collected. In running the credit union expenses are involved which use up some of the income. The *net earnings* for any given period (accumulating into undivided earnings yearly) are the amount by which the income exceeds the expenses in that period. Or a *loss* results if expenses exceed income. The business year for most credit unions is the same as their calendar year, but it can be any twelve-month period. Credit unions usually prepare financial statements showing their income and expenses for each calendar month, although the most important statement is that for the business year—the annual statement—which is a part of the treasurer's report to the members at their annual meeting.

Income and expense transactions are also recorded by debits and credits, on what might be called Temporary Accounts. The Temporary Accounts provide a chronological record of the activities of each year that shows whether the business operations of the credit union result in any added value to the members' shares. If there is any added value, it is owed to the members and eventually paid to them in dividends or other ways. Since each year's income and expense accounts are closed after they have served their purpose, they are called temporary or "nominal" accounts, as compared with the permanent or "real" asset and liability accounts that continue month after month as long as the credit union exists.

The credit union *credits* its *income* accounts for money it receives as interest on loans, or interest on any of its investments. It *debits* the *expense* accounts for money paid out for the various costs involved in operating the credit union, such as stationery, league dues, or insurance. Income adds to the assets of the credit union, and expenses reduce the assets. Sometimes expenses are not paid for in cash; instead the amount of the expense is owed to a creditor and, up to the time it is paid, is a liability of the credit union.

Here are some typical examples of income and expense transactions: The credit union credits its Interest-Income account for $1.00 when a member pays interest on his loan in that amount. It debits the Cash-in-Bank account for the same amount deposited in the bank.

Entry No. 5.　Debit—Cash in Bank　　$1.00
　　　　　　　　　Credit—Interest Income　　$1.00

The credit union purchases $15.00 worth of bookkeeping stationery from the league and pays for it with a check. The Expense account is debited for this addition to the cost of operating the organization, and Cash in Bank is credited to reduce the asset (Cash in Bank).

Entry No. 6.　Debit—Expense
　　　　　　　　　(Stationery)　$15.00
　　　　　　　　　Credit—Cash in Bank　　$15.00

Or on another occasion the credit union buys stationery from the league, but instead of paying cash for it, leaves the amount owing as a liability on an account payable to the league.

Entry No. 7.   Debit—Expense
                    (Stationery) $15.00
              Credit—Accounts Payable
                    (Credit Union League) $15.00

When the league account is paid with a check, the liability is reduced by a debit to the Accounts Payable while the asset account for Cash in Bank is reduced by a credit.

Entry No. 8.   Debit—Accounts Payable
                    (Credit Union League) $15.00
              Credit—Cash in Bank $15.00

THREE RULES

Let's pause for a refresher now and go back over these illustrations, with a few rules in mind. Like any other rules, these must be memorized, but maybe they will make more sense to us now that we have studied some actual examples of credit union bookkeeping transactions.

Rule No. 1: Every transaction of the credit union is recorded on its books and records in two parts, on opposite sides of an account—
    a debit—that goes on the left side
        and its opposite
    a credit—that goes on the right side
And for every transaction the debits must equal the credits.

Rule No. 2: The credit union keeps two sets of accounts: the Permanent Accounts show what the credit union, at any time, owns and what it owes, known as
    Assets (what the credit union owns)
            and
    Liabilities (what the credit union owes)
The Temporary Accounts, used on an accounting-period basis (usually annually) to show what income the credit union has taken in, and what expenses it has incurred, from the operation of its business, are known as

Income (what is received for the use of its money)
and
Expense (what is paid out to operate the business)

Rule No. 3: All of the accounts are increased or decreased by debits or credits, according to the theory that every transaction involves a value received and a value parted with, and thus results in adding to what the credit union owns or what it owes. Thus—

on the Permanent Accounts

Assets are increased by debits, signifying that a member or someone else owes something to the credit union. Assets are reduced by credits.

Liabilities are increased by credits, signifying that the credit union owes something to a member or someone else. Liabilities are decreased by debits.

on the Temporary Accounts

Expenses are increased by debits, signifying that the credit union has given up something of value, thus reducing what will be added to the value of the members' shares at the end of the business year.

Income is increased by credits, signifying that the credit union has received something that adds to the value of the members' shares and is therefore included in what is owed to the members.

CLOSING ENTRIES

At the end of the credit union's business year, which is usually the same as the calendar year, a special account called "Profit and Loss" is used to compute the earnings or loss resulting from the income and expenses of the year. All of the temporary—income and expense—accounts are closed by transferring their balances to Profit and Loss. If the credit union has earnings to show for its year's activity, some of these earnings are immediately set aside in a legally required or statutory reserve for losses on loans, or other reserves, according to the requirements of the bylaws of the credit union. The remainder of the earnings can be used for dividends on shares to pay the members for the use of their money during the year. If the computation shows that the earnings will be more than sufficient to build the reserves and to pay a reasonable dividend, some of the interest income can be returned to the borrowers who paid it during the year. This is known as an interest refund. All entries used for these year-end computations and transfers are called "closing entries."

These illustrated examples show how the bookkeeping entries appear in the Journal and Cash Record when the closing entries are made at the year-end:

Closing Entry A.

Debit—Interest Income	$446.00	
Credit—Profit and Loss		$446.00
Debit—Profit and Loss	$246.00	
Credit—Expenses		$246.00

(To close income and expense accounts to Profit and Loss)

Closing Entry B.

Debit—Profit and Loss	$40.00	
Credit—Statutory Reserve		$40.00

(To transfer 20% of net earnings to the statutory reserve)

Closing Entry C.

Debit—Profit and Loss	$160.00	
Credit—Undivided Earnings		$160.00

(To transfer remaining 80% of net earnings to undivided earnings)

Closing Entry D.

Debit—Undivided Earnings	$132.00	
Credit—Dividends Authorized		$132.00

(To record dividend authorized to be paid to members)

If the dividend is paid by crediting each member's share account with the amount of his dividend, another non-cash entry is made as follows:

Closing Entry E.

Debit—Dividends Authorized	$132.00	
Credit—Shares		$132.00

(To record payment of dividend by credits to the
members' share accounts)

Or, if the dividend is paid in cash to the members, the entries
would be:

Closing Entry E-1.

 Debit—Dividends Authorized $132.00
  Credit—Cash in Bank $132.00
   (To record payment of dividends in cash)

In actual practice none of the closing entries should be
made on the books of the credit union until after the treasurer
has computed on work papers the amount of the credit union's
earnings, the maximum amount of dividend that can be paid,
the amount of the actual dividend authorized by the board
of directors or by the membership, and the amount that may
be available for an interest refund.

For example, it can be seen from the Closing Entries A–C
that the credit union has $28.00 more than enough earnings
to pay the four percent dividend that had been authorized,
after the required transfer of earnings to the reserve account
has been made.

Interest Income	$446.00
Deduct: Expenses	— 246.00
Net earnings	$200.00
Deduct: 20% to statutory reserve	— 40.00
Undivided earnings	$160.00
Deduct: Dividend Authorized	— 132.00
Remaining undivided earnings	$28.00

Knowing this, the treasurer might recommend an interest
refund to be deducted from the Interest Income and returned
to the borrowers before closing entries are made as shown
above. A look at the Interest Income account shows that a
total of $446.00 was collected from borrowers during the
entire year. If $28.00 is left in the earnings after 20% of the
earnings have been transferred to reserve, then $28.00 equals
80% of the total earnings, $35.00, that would be available for
an interest refund if no such transfer were necessary. $35.00

Credit Union Assets Equal Liabilities

Whatever the credit union owns, it owes to its members*
Income minus expenses adds to ownership

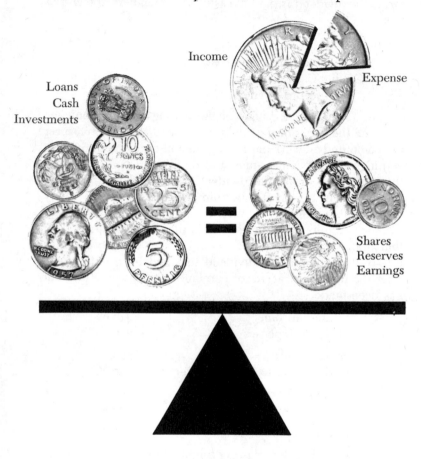

Income

Expense

Loans
Cash
Investments

Shares
Reserves
Earnings

ASSETS = LIABILITIES

*Except for borrowed money or expenses not paid for in cash.

works out to 7.8% of $446.00, but to simplify matters for everyone the treasurer might recommend that the amount of the interest refund be an even five percent. Each borrower would get back (either by credit to his share account or by payment in cash) exactly 5% of the total amount he had paid in interest to the credit union for the current year. The total amount of interest refunded would be $22.30. These entries would be made before any of the other closing entries.

Closing Entry F.

    Debit—Interest Income $22.30

        Credit—Interest Refund Authorized $22.30

        (To record authorization of 5% interest refund)

Closing Entry G.

    Debit—Interest Refund Authorized $22.30

        Credit—Cash in Bank $22.30

(To record payment of interest refund to member-borrowers in cash)

or

Closing Entry G-1.

    Debit—Interest Refund Authorized $22.30

        Credit—Shares $22.30

    (To credit interest refund to members' share accounts)

BOOKKEEPING STATIONERY USED BY CREDIT UNIONS

Except where government supervisory authorities specify the bookkeeping stationery to be used, credit unions are free to devise the forms best suited to their purposes. There is remarkable uniformity, nevertheless, and we can safely list some of the most commonly used bookkeeping stationery forms and a description of their use.

Cash Received Voucher—a short form on which the treasurer first records the date, member's name and passbook number, details of the credits for entrance fee, shares, loans, interest, or for any other purpose, and the total amount of the debit for cash received. The totals of all Cash Received Vouchers for a single day are summarized on a Summary Cash Received

Voucher, and these totals are carried to the appropriate columns on the Journal and Cash Record.

Collections Sheet—a full-page form on which the treasurer lists all cash collections, giving essentially the same information as the Cash Received Voucher. The Collection Sheet is especially convenient to use if no adding machine is available. It is also summarized at the end of each business day. Some credit unions, especially in the beginning stages when the officials are learning the steps in bookkeeping, use the Collections Sheet in addition to Cash Received Vouchers. However, either of the forms can be used without the other, since both contain the same information.

Cash Payment Voucher—a short form for recording the details of each transaction in which the credit union pays out cash and credits the Cash in Bank account. The date, member's name and passbook number, purpose of the payment to him, such as loan or withdrawal of shares, and amount of the debit to each account are included. Sometimes there is space for the member's signature or other signatures required to authorize the payment. This voucher can be used also for recording the amounts to be debited as expense payments. Cash Payment Vouchers can be summarized on a daily basis, but most credit unions issue each payment by check on the current bank account where the credit union deposits its money, and prefer to list each payment separately.

Journal and Cash Record—a chronological record of all cash received and paid out, usually made up of two pages to provide numerous columns for credits and debits to the various accounts involved in cash transactions. Usually cash receipts are entered in total amounts from the Summary Cash Received Voucher (or from the daily total of the Collections Sheet), and cash payments are entered individually from the Cash Payment Vouchers. This record is also the place where entries are made first to record non-cash transactions, such as adjustments, corrections of errors and closing entries. The monthly totals from the columns of the Journal and Cash Record are carried to the General Ledger.

General Ledger—the book of final entry, showing the assets, liabilities, income and expense accounts. The accounts are increased or decreased by the amounts transferred from the Journal and Cash Record. All other bookkeeping records serve to gather the figures which go into the General Ledger accounts, or act as supplementary records to these accounts. The financial statement is made up from the general ledger account balances at the end of each month.

In addition to the forms already described, these forms are used especially for the *information of the member or about the members:*

Application for Membership—sometimes known as the Signature Card, this form enables the member to supply facts about himself and his family which enable the credit union to determine whether he is eligible for membership, and to service his account after he becomes a member. His signature, next of kin, birth date, and address are usually requested. Where the law requires the credit union to maintain a membership register, this form can be adapted to that purpose as well, giving the legally required information for such a register. Usually these cards are filed in alphabetical order of the member's surname.

Member's Individual Share and Loan Ledger—one of these forms is used for each member, to record his name, address, passbook number and details of his share and loan transactions with the credit union, including the balance of shares credited to him, or loan for which he is a debtor; also memorandum information about the due dates of his loan payments or other loans for which he is responsible as a co-maker or guarantor. Information shown on this ledger comes from the Cash Received Vouchers and the Cash Payment Vouchers. It is identical to the information shown on the Member's Passbook.

Member's Passbook—as its name implies, this is the record given to the member showing his transactions with the credit union. Passbooks are issued in numerical order; the number is assigned permanently to the member. The passbook is the personal property of the member and often regarded as the "key" to his account, since most credit union bylaws require the member to present his passbook whenever he pays money into the credit union or receives money from the credit union. The entries in the passbook should be identical to those in the Individual Shares and Loan Ledger, so that these two records may be periodically checked against each other when audits are made.

When a member applies for a loan two additional forms are of great importance:

Application for Loan—on which the member supplies information needed by the credit committee to determine whether or not he should be granted a loan. An approved application is authorization for the treasurer to disburse the loan. This form is a permanent record of the credit union, retained as a record of every loan for which application has been made, including those not approved.

Promissory Note—the legal document suitable to the locality where it is used, which contains the promise of the member to repay his loan and, in addition to his signature, the signatures of his co-makers or guarantors who promise to pay if he should fail. When the loan is fully repaid, the Promissory Note is returned to the member or to his co-makers if they paid the loan for him.

As we come to the end of Part I in this chapter, we realize that an understanding of the bookkeeping system adds to our ability to understand the financial statement of a credit union. Knowing something about assets and liabilities, and income and expense, prepares us to strip the mystery from the financial statement and to observe what it has to tell us about the financial health or weakness of the credit union. We are not prepared at this point to keep the books of a credit union— more specific instructions are needed and can be found in any number of accounting manuals and treasurer's guides—but we have an idea of how the transactions of the credit union appear on the bookkeeping records and eventually on the financial statement. We have been looking at the financial workings of the credit union from the inside. Now it is time to take a look —a searching and critical look—from the outside.

FINANCIAL AND STATISTICAL REPORT
BEFORE CLOSING

For Period Ended _____, 19 _____ Charter No. _____

CREDIT UNION

Address _____

Street and Number   City - State

BALANCE SHEET				STATEMENT OF INCOME AND EXPENSE			
ACCT. NO.	ASSETS		END OF THIS MONTH	ACCT. NO.	INCOME	THIS MONTH	FROM TO DATE
101	Loans:	NUMBER	UNPAID BALANCES	401	Interest on Loans		
	DELINQUENT:			405	Income from Investments		
(a)	2 months to 6 months			406	Gain on Sale of Bonds		
(b)	6 months to 12 months			409	Other Income		
(c)	12 months and over						
	Subtotal						
(d)	Current and less than				Total Income		
	2 months delinquent	188					
(e)	Total Loans				EXPENSES		
				202-1	Treasurer's Salary		
104-105 106	Cash on Hand and in Banks			202-2	Other Salaries		
				202-3	Borrowers' Insurance		
				202-4	Life Savings Insurance		
107	U.S. Government Obligations			202-5	League Dues		
108	Savings and Loan Shares			202-6	Surety Bond Premium		
109	Loans to Other Credit Unions			202-7	Examination Fees		
112	Furniture, Fixtures and Equipment			202-8	Supervision Fee		
113	Unamortized Organization Cost			202-9	Int. on Borrowed Money		
114	Prepaid Insurance			202-10	Stationery and Supplies		
115	Other Assets			202-11	Cost of Space Occupied		
				202-12	Educational Expense		
				202-13	Collection Expense		
				202-14	Depreciation Furn., Fix. and Equip.		
				202-15	Social Security Taxes		
	Total Assets			202-16	Other Insurance		
				202-17	Recording Fees Chattel Lien Ins.		
	LIABILITIES AND CAPITAL			202-18	Communications		
301	Accounts Payable			202-19	Losses on Sale of Bonds		
302	Notes Payable			202-20	Cash Over and Short		
304	Withholding Taxes Payable			202-21	Other Losses		
305	Social Security Taxes Payable			202-22	Bank Service Charge		
333	Unempl. Comp. Tax Payable			202-	Unempl. Comp. Tax		
310	Shares						
311	Regular Reserve		6,108.08				
316	Special Reserve for Delinquent Loans						
318	Reserve for Contingencies			202-30	Misc. General Expense		
312	Undivided Earnings		1,385.01		Total Expenses		
313	Gain or Loss		7,565.10		Net Earnings		
	Total Liabilities and Capital				Net Loss		

STATISTICAL INFORMATION

ITEM		NUMBER	AMOUNT	ITEM		AMOUNT
1	No. of accounts at end of period			5	Loans charged off since organization	
2	No. of potential members	760	X X X X X X	6	Recoveries on loans charged off since organization	
3	Loans made year to date		X X X X X X	Certified correct by:		
4	Loans made since organization					

Treasurer

PART II

Financial Statement

As an essential control for supervisory purposes, government regulations are likely to require the use of a specific form for financial statements that must be submitted to the government; otherwise each credit union is free to use the form best suited to its purposes, in most localities, provided that it contains the essential information. The type of business organization we have in the credit union determines what is needed essentially: a statement of income and expense; a balance sheet; and statistical data to help interpret the preceding financial facts. Many possibilities exist for adding still more information, but let us keep in mind that we want every member to read the financial statement and to understand what he is reading. So in the interests of simplicity, our choice of a financial statement will be one that shows only the essential facts in an easily understandable form.

Our choice is the Financial and Statistical Report (Form FCU 109 Rev 6 62) illustrated on page 120. This report is used by many thousands of credit unions and, with some improvements in the statistical information, it could well become a world-wide favorite in many countries.

MAYBEE CREDIT UNION

To provide all the background information needed for our "specimen" credit union would require a chapter in itself. While the data shown on the Financial and Statistical Report of the Maybee Credit Union are taken from published statistics, using averages from the reports of many thousands of credit unions, we know that there is no such thing as an "average" credit union. Therefore the name "Maybee Credit Union."

Here are a few facts about it. Organized under state charter by employees of the Maybee Manufacturing Company in the United States on October 9, 1957, the credit union has a field of membership that includes employees of the company, members of their immediate families, and organizations of such persons. The average weekly wage of the employees is $110 and employment has been fairly steady for the past five years. The company does not provide payroll deductions for payments to the credit union. For the past seven years the credit union has paid an annual dividend of not less than 4%; this year the directors favor payment of a 10% interest refund; the amount of the dividend on 1965 shares has not yet been declared, but the Undivided Earnings are sufficient to pay a 5 percent dividend also. Although it has the legal right to accept deposits from its members, only share accounts have been accepted since the credit union first started.

The financial and statistical report is an indicator of the objectives, if any, which have been set by the board of directors of this credit union and of the success the credit union has had in reaching its objectives. Since we are not able to see the minutes of the annual membership meetings, or the board minutes, we must let the report speak for itself. However, since most credit unions have the same basic purposes and operate under very similar laws and bylaws, we might set the general direction of our analysis by recalling the principles set out at the beginning of this book:

> Membership that takes in as many potential members as possible
>
> Savings service that is convenient
>
> Ownership that goes with savings
>
> Loans tailored to the needs of the borrowers, granted with sympathy and understanding, and collected with firmness
>
> Interest charged at the maximum legal rates until experience shows the wisdom of reductions, by type of loan, or overall by interest refunds
>
> Dividends paid at reasonable rates
>
> Efficient operations
>
> Association with others in a credit union league or federation

How does the Maybee Credit Union measure up to these objectives?

FLOW OF INFORMATION
Through Credit Union Bookkeeping Records

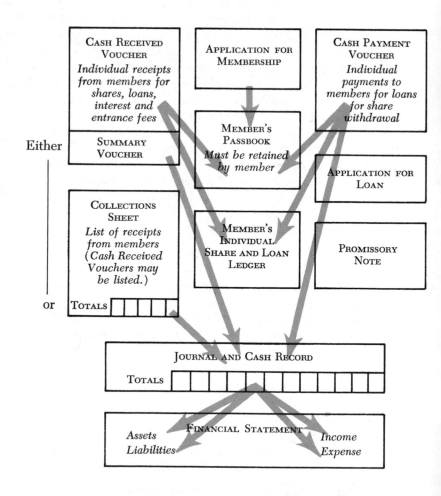

Making an Analysis of the Financial Statement

Membership That Takes in as Many Potential Members as Possible

According to Statistical Information Item 1 there are 401 accounts, and the potential membership according to Item 2 is 760, indicating that at best the credit union has enrolled only 52% of its potential members. That is far from a good record after over nine years of operation. It may be even less favorable depending on whether some members have more than one account, and on whether the families—wives, sons, daughters—of the Maybee employees who are also within the field of membership are included in the number of potential members. Normally they are not added to the number of company employees in arriving at the number of potential members. If some of these persons are members of the credit union, included in the 401 members reported, then the credit union has reached even less than 53% of its basic potential membership.

Perhaps if we search deeper into the financial and statistical report we can discover some of the reasons for this weakness. Is the credit union service adequate and is it convenient? Does the credit union work at the job of getting new members? Does it communicate on a regular basis with all members and potential members to get their ideas on improvements that would attract those who have decided not to join?

Looking at Items 3 and 4, it is evident that loans are being made on a reasonably active basis and $637, the size of the average loan made in 1965 ($167,727 ÷ 263 = $637) was large enough to meet some of the consumer loan needs of a worker making $110 per week. In previous years the loans were obviously much smaller because the average size of all loans made since organization was only $385. Perhaps in its earlier years the credit union was not able to grant loans large enough to help many of the employees consequently, even though it is now in a position to make larger loans and does make them, it has to overcome a mistaken concept or "image" that was created years ago. This is partly a problem in communications.

Does the credit union communicate? Let's turn to the statement of income and expense and look at the expenses that may give us a clue. The treasurer's salary at $1,800 and other salaries, $398, disclose that at United States annual wage scales it is obvious that the credit union is not paying any one person enough to hire a full-time employee. Cost of space occupied, $453, is probably enough to pay rent for modest office space, maybe on the company premises, but communications, $40, would possibly be just barely enough to pay for a telephone in the office. More likely the $1.33 communications expense for this month (December 1965) indicates that the credit union does not have its own telephone, but may share the cost with someone else in the office. The credit union office should be a place where potential members and members may transact their savings and loan business and discuss their problems with the treasurer, either in person or by telephone, and in reasonable privacy. But a better office would cost more money, and where would that money come from? The answer will appear later in our analysis.

There are other ways to communicate than in person or by telephone. Mailings of promotional and educational material on a regular schedule can be very effective in building membership. In the item for stationery and supplies expense of $230.05 there may be included some of these materials, or more likely they are included in the educational expense total of $60.92 for the entire year. Is this enough to do the job right, or does it indicate sporadic attempts to publicize the credit union now and again in bursts of activity?

The $200 in miscellaneous general expense for the annual meeting is a hopeful sign that the elected officials are determined to encourage good attendance at this important meeting. If the meeting is well planned and if the members will voice their opinions freely, the credit union leaders may find the answers to this problem of communications and membership. Perhaps they will learn that the members want more services, a better office—even their own building—and they are willing to support a program that will build the credit union to its full potential.

Savings Service That Is Convenient

On the balance sheet, under liabilities and capital, we find the total shares owned by 401 accounts of $142,101.22, an average of $354 per account, for the younger and older members, the low-paid and the high-paid. Factory workers with average pay in the United States cannot be expected to have large savings accounts in the years when they are raising their families, but systematic savings can work wonders. A credit union member who saves only one dollar a week has $52.00 in a year, and over a period of 8 years he would have $416. Every group of factory employees includes some who can save much more than the average. They put their money where it is safe, where it earns a reasonable dividend, and where it brings them other benefits—including the satisfaction of knowing that their money is working for the good of the group they belong to. The Maybee Credit Union has paid dividends of at least 4% for the past five years, it provides loan protection and life savings insurance as can be seen from the expenses, and it has made over a million dollars in loans to its members. All of this reflects good management and safety. Why, then, would the members with more savings to invest not bring those savings to the credit union? Perhaps they do not think of the credit union with its bare office as being a place to save more than a few dollars, perhaps there are restrictive policies that discourage saving in substantial amounts, and perhaps they prefer to save their money where it can help them obtain larger loans than the credit union has been granting.

How to make savings service more convenient? Payroll deduction would help but it is not the only answer. If the credit union could have a presentable office in which the members would feel the pride of ownership, if the office were open for business every day so that members could transact their business at times convenient to themselves, if there were some more tangible indications that the credit union is really a permanent organization and not just a side-activity connected with the industrial-relations office of the company where the members work, then perhaps this kind of service would attract new members and more savings from all members.

Ownership That Goes With Savings

It is not enough to point out that all of the shareholders who have the 401 accounts are owners of the credit union. They—the shareholders—must understand that they are owners of a credit union with total assets of $162,288.42; with unlimited potential for helping themselves and their families to make their savings productive not only in the form of loans, but also in building their own organization where a total range of financial services and financial counselling is within their reach. This kind of understanding comes with time, but it does not come unless a continuous educational program is carried on to tell the members what they have accomplished through their credit union and what they can accomplish with more effort. It is surprising to find how many credit union members lack any understanding of the cooperative structure of their organization, how many of them, especially in employee groups, think of the credit union as merely a personnel service provided by the employer.

Loans Tailored to the Needs of the Borrowers, Granted with Sympathy and Understanding, and Collected with Firmness

The Balance Sheet shows in the Assets section that there are 201 loans outstanding at December 31, 1965, with total unpaid balances of $120,503.40. Thus, almost exactly half of the share accounts have a loan. As we have noted, the average loan in 1965 was made for about $637. Not bad for a small-loan service. But is it good? Today's wage earner usually buys his auto and his household furnishings on the installment plan, in other words he borrows to pay for these expensive acquisitions. And he borrows to meet medical expenses, educational expenses, even recreational expenses. His debts with other lending or financing agencies are almost certain to cost him more interest than they would at his credit union. Loans for any of these purposes today are sizable. In fact, the average size of all loans made by federal credit unions in the United States in 1964 was $805.

It is questionable to say the least whether the Maybee Credit Union is granting loans that are tailored to the needs of its borrowing members. Perhaps the members do not think of approaching the credit union for all of their loan needs, even though they have always been treated with sympathy and understanding.

The Delinquent Loans as shown on the Balance Sheet number only 13 and amount to $5,853, of which the greatest number and amount (10 with unpaid balances of $4,734.01) are two months to 6 months delinquent. The Regular Reserve has $7,621.10 to meet any losses from uncollectible loans. After 9 years of operation the total amount of loans charged off as uncollectible (Statistical Information, Items 5 and 6) is $4,417.14, of which $714.02 has been recovered. The net loss of $3,703.12 is 31/100 of one percent of the total loaned since organization ($3,703 ÷ $1,196,614), very close to the industry average for all credit unions and a very good record indeed, reflecting a firm collection policy that achieved good results without the help of payroll deductions. We are not being unduly critical, however, to ask whether a more liberal lending policy that answers more closely to the needs of the members is now desirable even though it may increase the losses that are charged to the reserve. After all, the reserve is established specifically for the purpose of covering losses on uncollectible loans.

Interest Charged at Maximum Legal Rates until Experience Shows Wisdom of Reductions, by Type of Loan, or Overall by Interest Refunds

Here the answer is clear. We know that the credit union charges the maximum legal rate of interest—1% on the unpaid balance—on all loans, and judging from the Income—Interest on Loans in the Statement of Income and Expense—it appears that the credit union is collecting interest currently with loan collections. The Interest on Loans of $1,120.45 this month indicates that the outstanding loan balances at the end of the previous month were in the neighborhood of $112,000 (1% of $112,045.00 = $1,120.45), and the total Interest for the entire year $11,930.44, indicates that the outstanding loans averaged $99,420 for the year ($11,930.40 = 12% of $99,420.00). Loans have been increasing since the first of the year, apparently, along with shares.

The decision to pay an interest refund of ten percent is pertinent, because it shows that the board of directors is trying to find the answer to the problem of surplus funds. A higher dividend than 4 percent could be paid, but the pressures at this time are all on the side of encouraging more loans, not more savings. Does this justify the use of the interest refund for loan-promotion purposes alone? Not at all. In fact the board of directors may be puzzled next year when savings come in at a faster rate than ever before, induced in part by the announcement that the credit union has paid its first interest refund. Success in any of its activities is a spur to more membership participation in the credit union, more savings, and also more borrowing.

The advantage of the interest refund at this particular time is that it fits in with the principle of returning all earnings to the members; it reduces the earnings for 1965, thus reducing the amount added to the reserve that is already more than adequate; and it can be the "opening gun" in a campaign to put the credit union on a full-service program.

Dividends Paid at Reasonable Rates

Any credit union that has paid dividends consistently since its second full year of operations, always at the rate of 4% or better, is doing as well as the majority of all credit unions everywhere and that is commendation enough. We know that the Maybee Credit Union also provides two forms of life insurance for the benefit of its members, Loan Protection Insurance and Life Savings Insurance. The Statement of Income and Expense shows these as Expenses respectively in the yearly amounts of $600.11 and $650.09, which total to $1,250.20. This is probably equivalent to at least a 1% dividend on the average shares owned by the members during the entire year.

With imagination and skillful management, the credit union members could probably provide other benefits for themselves that might outweigh the amounts they receive as dividends. With fulltime operation and participation in the services and programs offered by the league to which it pays dues, the credit union might provide a financial counselling service that would save members substantial money on their most important purchases, show them how to budget their income to make each dollar go farther, and raise their sights to the challenge of other cooperative activities that would benefit the entire community.

Efficient Operations

The Statement of Income and Expense tells much about the various strengths and weaknesses of credit union management, as we have observed. Now we find the crucial ratio of operating efficiency: Total Expenses as a percent of Total Income. If the acid test of management of a financial institution is its ability to pay a dividend on the capital, this expense ratio is a reliable indicator of whether management in a particular credit union can meet the test. Data are now published by CUNA International, Inc., a number of credit union leagues, and the Bureau of Federal Credit Unions that include operating ratios and averages for credit unions of various size groups, age groups, or field-of-membership groups. These data permit analyses that disclose why some credit unions have lower expense ratios than others.

The Maybee Credit Union has an expense ratio of 42% (Total Expenses $5,542 ÷ Total Income $13,107). In the experience of most credit unions, a 50% expense ratio is essential for adequate services and safety of operations, but credit unions can be fully self-supporting and provide more than average service while maintaining an expense ratio of less than 50%. The 42% expense ratio and the business-like accounting for proportionate parts of most expenses each month show that the examination fees paid each year ($288.13 for 1965) were well spent. No doubt the advice and guidance given by the government examiner have been helpful to the credit union.

There is more to efficient operations, however, than achieving a favorable relation between income and expense. Usually a credit union is efficient if it is a full-service credit union, one which reaches out for every member, every savings dollar, every loan that can be made, and tries to render every service which the members want and which can be provided under the provisions of its charter. To build a full-service credit union the members and particularly the leaders must grow with the changing times. They must literally stretch their minds to think of all that the members can do for themselves through their credit union. Procedural or legal obstacles may inhibit such thinking. An understanding of the benefits at stake should help the members decide whether or not it is worth the effort to build a full-service credit union.

The Maybee Credit Union has Total Assets of $162,288.42 of which $120,503.40 or 74% of the Total Assets is working directly for the members in Loans. Surplus funds invested in Savings and Loan Shares alone amount to $25,504.00 or 15% of Total Assets. These funds invested in loans to members would bring 12% per year; the credit union probably receives 4½%—more or less—on this money. Cash on Hand and in Banks amounts to $13,533.02 or 8% of Total Assets, earning nothing and in fact probably subject to Bank Service Charges as shown by the Expense item of $24.10 under this heading, on the Statement of Income and Expense. Some of the cash could and probably will be used to pay off the Liability of Notes Payable, $4,130.00, at the opportune time for the credit union, after the heavy demand for cash passes following the Christmas and New Year Holidays.

With so much surplus money employed at less than full efficiency the question arises: How to put this surplus to work for the credit union? One solution is implied in all of our preceding discussion—set new goals for a full-service credit union, with fulltime operations, an attractive office, new services that recognize all the needs of today's wage earner, the courage to experiment and a willingness to learn from the experience of others.

Association with Others in Credit Union League or Federation

League dues of $272.02 for 1965 appear among the Expenses on the Statement of Income and Expense. The Balance Sheet items Loans to Other Credit Unions, $1,067.00, and Notes Payable, $4,130.00, suggest interlending activities possibly helped by the league. These are healthy signs of the willingness to associate with other credit unions, but they do not necessarily mean that the elected officials have the willingness to learn from others. Unless the leaders of the credit union take part in league activities, and use its services, they are not getting full value for the dues paid. Does the league offer consulting services, management surveys, promotional advice? Has a representative of the league ever been invited to meet with the board of directors and discuss the concepts of a full-service program? Or has any member of the elected management attended one of the meetings sponsored by the league where other credit union leaders are present, friendly people who will consider it a privilege to help another credit union? There are no trade secrets among the credit unions. Belonging to the league implies participation in the community of credit unions, giving and receiving help that is possible only within that community. Such participation usually leads to more involvement in the entire community of business and civic organizations, bringing better understanding on all sides.

. . . .

We have barely touched upon the most obvious points involved in the analysis of a credit union financial statement. Experience will indicate where more attention should be given to the tell-tale signs of weakness in a particular credit union. The Maybee Credit Union is a good credit union as compared with many others, but pertinent criticisms coming from its own members might help make it a better credit union. As the members learn more about the social and economic theory, and about the practice of credit union operations, they will be better prepared to offer helpful criticism.

It is essential for credit union officers and other elected officials to understand their own credit union's financial statement. Skill in the analysis of credit union financial statements should be a pre-requisite for anyone aspiring to the higher levels of credit union management or government supervisory responsibility.

VIII

Man and His Money

What Is Money and Why Is It Important?

Money—to most of us—means dollars, shillings, pesos, francs, deutsche marks, pounds, rubles, sucres, pesetas or any of the monetary units, of currency and coins, designated by the countries of the world for use in their monetary systems. It could just as well be anything of recognized value which men agree to use for the payment of goods, services or debts— the wampum of early American Indians, the 200-pound stones once used on the Island of Yap in the South Pacific, or the cattle of the Masai tribes in East Africa who even today measure their wealth by the size of their herds.

Money in the form of tokens is issued by governments or government agencies, or by banks with governmental approval. Usually it represents the ownership of precious metals such as gold or silver which people of the country and the nations of the world recognize as having universal value. The coins or the paper currency in our pockets have little value in themselves—gold coins are almost non-existent, most so-called silver coins have practically no silver content, and coins of other metals would not be worth melting down for the value of the metals in them. We think of the paper bills, notes and other forms of paper currency as having value because the government of our country says they are worth the amounts shown, and because other people in our country and other countries will accept them at this value.

In the United States and many other countries money is also based on credit. When a bank makes a loan to one of its customers the credit extended on that loan, the promise of the customer to repay the loan with interest, is recognized as being "as good as gold." With the approval of the government of the United States, commercial banks belonging to the federal reserve system have the power to create new money within certain limits, based partly on the savings deposited by their customers, and partly on the value of the promissory notes of their customers. When this new money is created it is not always necessary to issue currency and coins, because in the United States, as in so many other countries, business transactions are accomplished by issuing checks or other forms of written authorizations for the transfer of money from one account to another. In fact, most of the money created by the commercial banking system of the United States is "checkbook money," involving only the bookkeeping entries to record the credits on the accounts of the borrowing party in his bank account. Checks drawn on the account are as good as any other kind of money.

The Federal Reserve Board also has the power to set the basic interest rate on money throughout the country by setting the interest rate that banks must pay to the Federal Reserve banks. This rate determine what banks charge and it influences the rate other lenders—who use bank credit—will charge.

Access to Credit Is Important to Everyone

Obviously, a bank or agency that can create money in this way and can set the price on it is very powerful. The power to create the money with which to give credit to a businessman in need of a loan to stock his inventory periodically, or to expand his business by additions of machinery, buildings or work force, literally exerts the power of life and death over his business. So is the power to create money for a farmer's seasonal seed and fertilizer requirements, or for the purchase of more acreage, or for farm machinery.

Both the big business community and the big farm operators are extremely important to the welfare of any country.

Except for historic periods of extreme business depression, they have managed to get the money and credit they need through the commercial banks, or through special agencies of government that lend government money direct or through the commercial banks. They have balanced the power of the banks with their own political power to influence government. Sometimes they have gotten control of banks or influenced their policies by buying up decisive amounts of stock.

Wage earners, salaried employees, small businessmen and subsistence farmers have not been so fortunate. They have been unable to bargain effectively for the right to use some of the money created by the banks. Their own savings in those same banks were not generally available to them in loans, because it was more profitable for the banks to use their money, both the money they obtained from these savings and the additional money they created on the basis of these savings, to make loans to sales finance companies, small loan companies, and other businesses that specialize in financing household purchases and expenses. More recently the banks have gone into the small-loan business themselves.

High Cost of Credit

Interest charges have taken a heavy toll of the worker's income, whenever he has used the services of those who are in business to make a profit from lending. The entire economy of a country shares in the loss of this income, and there is even more to be lost when workers are unable to get any credit on reasonable terms. The ambition of families to become more productive is encouraged only when they are able to get better homes, better education, better medical care and better transportation.

This is not just a problem of our times. It is the age-old problem of man through the centuries of recorded history. Egyptians and Greeks long before our era, have left us with descriptions of money-lending abuses as have the people of biblical times, abuses so serious that the Book of Exodus commands—"If thou lend money to any of My people, even to the poor with thee, thou shalt not be to him as a creditor; neither shall ye lay upon him interest." (Exodus 22:24)

The high cost of credit is still a problem in both the most advanced and the most primitive countries in the world. Twenty-five years ago an assistant attorney general of the state of Massachusetts wrote a book about his experiences in which he told in detail about the abuses of loan sharks, both legal and illegal money lenders, who operate outside of the law and within the legal limits as well, to squeeze extortionate interest out of the people least able to pay.* Today as in the 1930's the big cities of the United States are plagued by the "juice racket," just another name for illegal money lending, run by gangsters and hoodlums who find it more profitable than any of their other rackets.

In Peru the Incas of the 13th to 16th centuries are known to have had a credit system, through which the government advanced credit to help newlyweds buy land and erect houses for their homes. In our times the Indians who are descendants of those same Incas are unable to get loans from banks because it is against the Peruvian law. Usurers have been the only source of credit for improving their land, or for any other purpose, and they charge interest at 10 to 50 percent per year. In the Philippines a typical farm family consisting of a farmer, his wife, and their six children lives on an income of approximately 150 pesos a year, or about $50.00. When there is a crop failure the farmers are at the mercy of money lenders who get up to 400% interest for small loans.

A typical Bolivian farmer may spend his entire life settling a debt of less than $100 to pay for surgical attention to his child, because the going interest rate of the loan sharks there is 10 percent per month, or 120 percent a year. In Fiji where most of the natives are farmers and fishermen, a majority of them do not own even as much as a fishing net after a lifetime of work. The reason? Nets are rented by the day; failure to bring in a catch of fish means no money to pay the rent, and high-rate interest accumulates on the debt. Many fishermen are lucky to keep up with their interest payments, and loans for improving their farms or buying farm tools are out of the question.

*Goldman, Maurice, *You Pay and You Pay*. New York: Howell, Soskin & Co., 1941.

In the new Republic of Tanzania, East Africa, loans for funeral expenses, or for the cost of celebrating births and weddings were not condoned by the civil authorities in colonial times, and even today they are not available to most people except through friends or members of the family. It takes at least 300 shillings ($42.00) for the bride price. The cost for a loan in the rural areas of Tanzania from a local moneylender is 5 shillings for 100 shillings borrowed, per week, or 260 percent per year. In Nairobi, Kenya, it is 1,300%—5 shillings for every ten shillings each two weeks.

Money is like any other commodity. It has a price. When it is plentiful the price goes down and when it is scarce the price rises. The price we are speaking of is *interest*. When loans are hard to get, lenders raise their interest rates but the borrower, especially if he is in great need, is glad to pay any price asked. If he cannot get a loan from a legal lender who is subject to some limitations on what he is permitted to charge, the needy borrower will go to anyone who has money to lend and pay whatever interest is demanded. This is what makes usury possible.

Depending on the circumstances, the interest rate that in one place or at one time may be unreasonable, may become reasonable at another time or place. No one would argue with calling the "juicers" usurers—they get $1.00 for $5.00 per week, or 1,040% per year. But is it fair to lump all pawnbrokers into the same category as usurers because their legally permitted rates are high: 24%–30%? Considering the relative risk and the cost of providing the service, it might be just as accurate to label other loan agencies as usurers for charging up to 42% on small loans, 18%–30% for financing household appliances, or 18%–34% for financing the purchase of second-hand autos. Even higher rates result when the purchaser pays ahead of schedule but receives no reduction in the amount of interest that has been charged in advance or "discounted."

The remedy for usury is not legislation although making it illegal has had some effect on usurious lending. There is a much more direct way of discouraging usury, and that is to give people a source of credit at reasonable rates, or at least some way to check the prices on credit among the various lenders.

Why Credit Unions Make a Difference

There is a fundamental difference between a credit union and any commercial money lender. It is quite simply the difference between people's doing with their own savings what is best for themselves, and people's giving up those savings to others whose main aim is to make a profit. In the credit union, all the capital from which the credit is made possible comes from the members and the earnings on that money belong to the members. They have no reason to deceive themselves as to the cost. In a commercial bank or other financial agency using other people's money, the owners invest a relatively small amount of their own money to operate a lending business which depends on using large amounts of other people's money. The profits from this lending go to the owners of the bank, the loan company or the sales finance agency, and profit-making is the ultimate objective.

It is reassuring to belong to a credit union where surplus earnings are returned as dividends on the member's shares, returned as interest refunds to the borrowers who paid the interest, or set aside in reserves to protect the share value of the members. Some credit unions make reductions in the interest rate charged on all loans or on certain types of loans if they find from experience that this is preferable to interest refunds, and results in giving better service.

Shopping for Credit

There is another reason credit unions make a difference, which involves the fundamental question of whether the purchaser of money—the man who uses credit—is entitled to know what price he is paying for his credit.

In more and more countries industrial and social progress has brought the comforts of civilization within the reach of many more people. The technology of these countries is geared to mass production of consumer goods and personal services which must be used up so that the system can continue to function. The consumer has become important because his purchases are essential to the system. The amount he buys of goods and services and the intervals between those purchases determine whether factories and service organizations will stay in business and whether there is prosperity, inflation or depression. A goodly supply of money and credit keeps this type of consumer economy going. In fact, the lending agencies must compete with each other to induce the consumer to borrow from them.

In Canada and the United States up to the early 1900's lending to business was considered productive, and banks competed to some extent for business loans and the profits to be made from them. After that date the needs of the worker for credit began to be recognized and a succession of other lenders, specialized agencies, came into operation to meet these needs. In 1909 the credit unions got started; in 1910 Morris Plan Banks (workers' industrial banks) were introduced to encourage savings and to lend to workers at lower rates; in 1911 the first small-loan laws were passed to encourage personal-finance companies to lend money at more reasonable rates than were generally available; and much later, after World War II, the commercial banks plunged into consumer lending with all their resources. In more recent years England and Europe have developed similar consumer economies, and the same type of development is emerging all over the world.

It was estimated that at the end of 1965 the people of the United States alone were indebted for $65 billion of consumer credit which was costing them 22 cents out of every dollar of income after taxes. The mounting numbers of personal bankruptcies attest to the fact that many Americans are using more credit than they can afford. Obviously the profits to be made from this business are very great, and since the borrower is going to pay for getting this service he should know what price he is paying when he borrows from the different lending agencies.

There are few choices open to people who are struggling to subsist in a country which is in the early stages of development. Money is scarce and everyone tries to get his share of it. Cost of the money is a secondary and minor consideration, even though excessive cost may take a terrible toll eventually in loss of production, prolonged poverty, profiteering and social degredation. Often these abuses are allowed to fester until, as in biblical days, strong measures are taken to bring some relief.

When a country builds its economy to the stage where subsistence is not the problem and many comforts are within reach the people have some choice as to how they will spend their money. Some of that money may come from savings. Much of it is likely to come from loans which must be repaid with interest out of the workers' earnings. For most purchases, the worker searches for goods or services he wants at the lowest price. He should be able to shop for his credit as he shops for his food and clothing.

Truth in Lending

Depending on the stage of a country's development, it may or may not be possible for people to have all the credit they would like. Whether credit is scarce, or whether it is plentiful, the borrower should know what he is paying for the credit he uses. Most financial agencies use one term among themselves to describe the price of credit, the cost of money, which is the commodity they buy and sell when they borrow or lend. That term is *simple interest* expressed as a percentage of the amount borrowed, which is the rate charged for a given period of time, normally one year. Thus *simple annual interest* is the total cost of using a given amount of money for one full year, stated as a percent of the money used. This measurement of the price of money is easily understood and easy to compute, and it works well for the institutions that engage in millions of transactions each year involving billions of dollars.

Some lenders, such as small loan companies and credit unions, state their rates in *simple monthly interest*. They charge interest only for the actual time the borrower has use of the money, but they compute the rate as a certain percent each month. This is readily converted to the annual rate by multiplying by twelve for the number of months in a year. The credit union rate of one percent per month is twelve percent per year (1% per month × 12 months = 12% per year). Other lenders, however, state their charges in terms that are very difficult to understand or to use for comparison. "Discount," "Add-on," "Service Charges," "Investigation Fees" and innumerable other labels are used to account for the interest charged to the borrower.

The problem becomes more complicated when the credit is not in the form of a money loan but part of a purchase agreement tied into the price of the article or service purchased. This type of credit "at the point of purchase" is becoming increasingly important. At 18% simple annual interest, the usual rate charged, this kind of credit is often more profitable than the sale of the merchandise on which it depends. This may help explain why reputable merchandisers, who are willing to give the consumer important facts about the quality and quantity of the goods he is buying, are reluctant to give him similar facts about the credit he is paying for.

Legislative action is under consideration both in Canada and in the United States to require all lenders to state the price of their credit in terms of simple annual interest, and credit unions are supporting Senator David Croll in Canada and Senator Paul Douglas in the U. S., the sponsors of this "Truth-in-Lending" legislation. In time, and as the public demands to know the truth, the other lending agencies and the merchandising firms who almost universally oppose it, may change their position.

Until the worker, the small businessman, and the farmer have a fair chance to learn what credit costs, one of their best protections against usury is the credit union.

Whenever the borrower can learn the total cost he is paying for credit—i.e. the finance charges—he can use this formula to find the annual simple interest rate:

$$r = \frac{2pd}{c(n+1)}$$

r = annual interest rate
p = number of payment periods in a year
d = total dollar cost of finance charges
c = amount of credit advanced
n = number of installments

Example:

Mr. Consumer buys a stereo phonograph on sale at $399.50. He makes a cash payment of $99.50, leaving $300 to be paid in 12 monthly installments on the "easy-payment plan." Each monthly payment is computed as follows:

	per month	per year
$300 ÷ 12	$25.00	$300.00
Add 10% Service Fee	2.50	30.00
Total payment	$27.50	$330.00

The 10% Service Fee turns out to be 18.4% simple annual interest:

$$\text{Annual interest rate} = \frac{2 \times 12 \times \$30}{\$300 \times (12 + 1)}$$

$$\text{Annual interest rate} = \frac{\$720}{\$3,900}$$

$$\text{Annual interest rate} = 18.4\%$$

CUNA Supply Cooperative also has an interest rate converter on which almost any kind of credit charges can be converted into simple annual interest.

Truth-in-Lending may never be accomplished by legislation. Far more effective than laws to require the disclosure of annual interest rates would be the education of borrowers in ways whereby they can get the maximum use out of their own money. There are historical reasons for believing that, although this may be difficult, it is very definitely possible.

Benefits to Credit Unions of Central Bank

When we recall that the commercial banks through the Federal Reserve system have the power to create money and to determine the basic-interest rate on money for the entire money-and-banking system of the United States, we marvel at the ability of the credit unions to maintain their same lending policies throughout periods of "easy money" and "tight money." It is even more remarkable that they have held their interest rates at a constant 12% for nearly sixty years. Thousands of credit unions have done even better: they have reduced those rates.

Unequal to the banks in size and strength, having no central fund through which to pool their resources, credit unions nevertheless have managed to exercise some control over their own money.

Yet, as long as they are without a central bank or fund, they exist as individual credit unions subject to the dangers of isolated units in times of financial stress. Despite the existence of a few multi-million-dollar credit unions, most of them are small. Total assets of all credit unions in the United States are less than the resources of any one of several giant banks. Should the time ever come when they might need money they could be seriously damaged if they were unable to raise the needed funds.

Today, while United States credit unions are being prodded to fight for the consumer-loan business and the savings of their members, a strange anomaly exists—over $1½ billion of the total $10 billion in assets is not working for credit union members. It is invested instead mostly in shares of savings-and-loan associations and to a lesser extent in certificates of deposit of commercial banks, who use this money for their own profit-making purposes. Credit union members feel fortunate to borrow their own money at an interest rate of 12% annually, but they are lending it to these rival institutions at 4% to 4½% or roughly one-third of the return it would bring to their credit union if they put it to work for themselves.

If Desjardins was right when he said "the people's welfare can best be secured by the institutions organized by the people themselves" the time has come to challenge the credit union movement with a more dynamic concept of service that will channel members' savings into more productive investments as well as give them more control over their own money. A central bank could launch the credit union movement toward new heights of growth and service. A central reserve system within the bank could protect the value of members' shares.

IX

History

Most of the books on the credit union bookshelf are devoted to biographical accounts of the pioneers of the credit union movement whose lives have made credit union history, and to the historical narrative of credit union activities in Europe and North America. To repeat that history in detail is beyond the scope of this chapter. Instead this chapter will be an attempt to interpret credit union historical developments—especially the events of the last thirty years in the United States—as an epoch in man's age-old struggle to become master of his own money.

Throughout this book we have been looking mostly at the individual credit union. We have sifted through numerous details of credit union management, social and economic functions, even bookkeeping, to gain an understanding of the credit union: what it is that makes it easy for men to get such astonishing results from combining the power of their most material resource, money, with the force of the completely intangible resources we call character, honesty and integrity. Now we take a sweeping glance at the entire picture, in which the central figures are the credit unions and their institutions, and ask ourselves, "What is the real significance of this credit union movement, historically, and in our times? What place will it have in the annals of mankind's universal quest for a fairer distribution of the world's wealth?"

In the few countries where cooperatives are still trying

to win acceptance, it is important for the historical origins of cooperative credit to be clearly understood so that people can make an intelligent choice among the institutions vying for their support. In the growing number of countries where cooperatives have widespread acceptance it may be more vital to ask whether there is reason to hope that from the successes of the credit union movement men can extend their achievements by international cooperation.

After all, credit unions trace their history to beginnings in many countries.

Credit unions were born of adversity. The problems of the poor today—the day laborer living in one of the slums of the big cities, in "the pockets of poverty," as they are called in the United States, or the peasant farmer scratching out a bare living with primitive tools in any of the new nations of Africa and Asia—are small problems compared to the utter hopelessness of the people who first tried the credit union idea. Apathy, despair and suspicion immobilized the people of Europe in the middle of the 19th century. The industrial revolution with its promise of a better life for all had brought misery to the dispirited factory workers in England. Much of Europe was suffering from the impact of the ruinous Napoleonic Wars and the revolutions of 1790–1848. A series of bad crop years in Germany, still an agricultural country, had left many of her people poverty-stricken and in debt. Even in the "Golden Land" as the United States was called, the "Hungry Forties" (1840–1850) sent waves of discontent through the immigrants who had come to their new homes with such high hopes.

The concepts of cooperation were new and untried, but they offered some outlet for the frustrations of jobless, hungry and discouraged people. Robert Owen, the Englishman, inspired the unemployed weavers of Rochdale to save $140 out of their few pennies and to start the first consumer's cooperative in 1844. In France the names of Buchez (1796–1865), Proudhon (1809–1865) and Louis Blance (1811–1882) appeared on writings about cooperatives. In Germany, Victor Huber (1800–1869) published a treatise "Credit Unions and Loan Unions." Francis Haeck in Brussels, Belgium, in 1848, founded a cooperative savings and loan association which he called a *boerenbond* or credit union.

As the theories of writers on cooperatives were put to the test of actual practice they seemed to work, and encouraged the pioneers to begin experiments in a number of countries. Trial and error exposed the weaknesses in the theories; observation and discussion among themselves helped the pioneer organizers to determine where changes had to be made.

Germany became the laboratory for some of the most important experiments in cooperative banking. Two men, each one gifted, tenacious and visionary, led the way. Both tried to help the people around them find a way to get the credit that was so sorely needed just to keep their families and themselves alive. Both are remembered today as the founders of the credit union movement. The principles of self-help, self-government, and self-responsibility have come down to us today from the societies they organized.

Herman Schulze, mayor of the town of Delitszch and usually known as Herman Schulze-Delitszch, tried to help the mechanics, craftsmen and small tradesmen in the towns and cities who needed credit to buy leather for the shoemaker, cloth for the tailor, tools for the carpenter—and a way to market their products cooperatively to compete with the big businesses. His efforts to get money from charitable people of wealth failed and he had little faith in the ability of the needy people to raise the money that was required. So he set up his societies with share capital and made the shares an attractive investment by insisting on efficient operations, compensation to employees and officers, high dividends, and loans for productive purposes only. When more money was needed, Schulze-Delitszch went to the commercial banks. He was fortified with another convincing proposition that answered their demands for security. The credit union members would be personally liable without limitation for all loans and other advances made to their credit union. Substantial funds started to flow in and, as the societies succeeded, they spread out through the country, sometimes as new credit unions and sometimes as new branches. Large membership was common. The members paid high entrance fees and bought high-priced shares on the installment plan, attracting more money from the banks, and eventually building their credit unions so strong that the requirement of unlimited liability could be invoked only occasionally. In his lifetime (1808–1883) Schulze-Delitszch was recognized as the founder of urban credit unions. The first credit union he organized in 1852 (he called it a bank) became the forerunner of a system of cooperative banks which still serves the people of Germany today.

Unfortunately, these credit unions never reached the people who were in greatest need, those too poor to pay the high entrance fees or to invest in costly shares, the penniless people. It took another leader to show that this could be done.

Frederick William Raiffeisen, mayor of the small village Flammersfeld in Southern Germany, was a deeply religious man, a lay Lutheran preacher. He was greatly troubled by the poverty of his people because he saw that for them, worse than having no food or clothing, was the resulting degradation, apathy and despair.

He recognized the logic of cooperation and believed deeply in the Biblical injunctions on charity and brotherhood of man. But when he tried to organize credit unions to help the poor farmers with funds provided by the rich, he encountered failure again and again. Raiffeisen's societies differed from those of Schulze-Delitszch whose urban credit unions were rapidly gaining strength: his societies had no entrance fees, no shares, paid no dividends. All savings and earnings went into one indivisible fund. Raiffeisen, finally, had to admit that nothing permanent could be built on charity. He accepted Schulze-Delitszch's argument that credit unions are best built on the principles of self-interest and self help, and strongly embraced the principle of unlimited liability. However, he found it particularly difficult to accept the business approach to loans that was helping to make the Schulze-Delitszch societies so successful. Throughout his lifetime Raiffeisen emphasized character as the best security for loans, and the moral responsibilities of credit unions for helping those least able to help themselves. The credit unions he founded were concerned as much with restoring drunkards and outcasts to productive society as they were with the business of cooperative banking. And they succeeded.

The first successful Raiffeisen Village Bank is believed to have started in 1864 in Heddesdorf. Hundreds of others were organized by Raiffeisen in the period from his earliest experiments in 1849 until his death in 1888. Whereas Schulze-Delitszch saw the uniformly successful achievements of his credit unions during his lifetime, many of the Raiffeisen experiments with agricultural cooperatives failed and most of the Raiffeisen development took place after his death. The principle of unlimited personal responsibility was a cornerstone for the Raiffeisen societies, and even today the motto *One for All and All for One* bespeaks this principle. It is one of the main strengths of the entire system of rural societies in Germany, be they credit, commodity or management societies, that owe their name and their origins to William Raiffeisen.

Raiffeisen demonstrated that cooperatives with a high social purpose can work successfully, not only in the field of banking but in every other economic area as well, a fact that has been emphasized all too infrequently—perhaps de-emphasized—in the American credit union movement. He is honored everywhere as a source of inspiration and guidance for modern credit unions. Some of the Raiffeisen society's practices are no longer followed in Germany or in other countries which started with his basic formula, but his ideas of a truly cooperative people's bank and his firm belief that helping people is more important than making a profit are still the guiding principles for the credit union movement around the world.

The credit union successes in Germany led to the organization of similar societies in Italy, which already had the *montes pietatis* (poverty banks) since medieval times. Luigi Luzzatti established the first credit union in Milan in 1866 after studying the Schulze-Delitszch societies, and his credit unions spread throughout the urban areas of Italy, developing improvements—low entrance fees, low-priced shares, unsecured loans, a reserve fund—which were later to guide American pioneers. He encouraged Leon Wollemborg to start a similar program for farmers, beginning in 1863, and the Italian rural credit union program again demonstrated to those watching European experiments that this concept of cooperative banks was exportable.

While the credit union idea was to travel many thousands of miles eastward during the next hundred years, western credit union development has excited more interest in our times. In Levis, Quebec, Canada, a parliamentary reporter and journalist named Alphonse Desjardins had been reading about the successful European cooperatives and corresponding with the noted cooperative leaders, Henry Wolff in England, Charles Gide in France and Luigi Luzzatti in Italy. After years of study and careful planning to construct the right model for a credit union of French Canadians, Desjardins decided that, as in Germany's rural areas, the parish was the best field of membership but, unlike any of the German credit unions, the money for share capital must come *entirely* from the members and it would be withdrawable on short notice.

In 1900 he organized the first Canadian credit union *Caisse Populaire de Levis.* His leadership led to the enactment of legislation that made it possible to charter *caisses populaires* anywhere in the province of Quebec. The *caisses populaires* of Canada, most of them in Quebec, were to grow rapidly and strongly like their counterparts in Germany and today they constitute one of the most powerful cooperative financial systems in the world. Desjardins laid the foundation for other credit unions throughout Canada, and in 1909 he also played an important part in establishing the first credit union, St. Marie Parish of Manchester, New Hampshire, and the first credit union law, in the United States.

The successes of the *caisses populaires* in Quebec did not go unnoticed in the United States. A few hundred miles south of Levis, at Boston, Massachusetts, where debt-ridden factory workers were finally able to make their complaints heard, an investigation had been ordered into the operations of professional money-lenders by the state banking commissioner, Pierre Jay. In 1908 he invited Desjardins to help draw up a bill legalizing credit unions in Massachusetts, and in 1909 the proposed law was submitted to the state legislature. Among those who testified in favor was Edward A. Filene, a wealthy and influential Boston merchant whose testimony in support so impressed the legislative committee that the bill was passed and signed into law on May 21, 1909.

While traveling in India, Filene had met a man by the name of W. R. Gourlay, who was employed by the British government to organize cooperative savings and loan societies among the desperately poor Indian farmers. These Indian credit unions were working remarkably well. Filene accompanied Gourlay on his visit for awhile, and in the successful Indian cooperatives he saw the answer to the money-lending abuses in his home state. The credit union idea had traveled half-way around the globe from Europe to India, and Filene brought it almost full circle—to the U.S.A.

Edward A. Filene (1860–1937) is remembered in many countries for his unusual ability to see, as few others of his time could visualize, that the prosperity of a country depends on putting purchasing power into the hands of its people. He was a humanitarian, interested in using his money to help other people, and his many projects in that direction had already won him world-wide recognition. From the moment he first encountered the credit union idea, Filene became increasingly involved with credit union development until that became the project closest to his heart.

After the passage of the Massachusetts credit union law in 1909, Filene continued to seek the help of other civic leaders and organizations in his efforts to get credit union legislation in other states. In 1908 President William Howard Taft sent a letter to the governor of every state suggesting credit union legislation, and this gave support to the efforts of Filene. People in other states were showing definite interest, but there was no uniformity in their thinking and no direction to their efforts. Only four states, Massachusetts, New York, Rhode Island and North Carolina had effective credit union laws. By 1921 Filene decided that the way to get the kind of results he wanted from this project was to create a national organization for the sole purpose of putting credit unions within the reach of everyone in the United States. His choice to head the organization, in fact to *be* the organization when it was getting started, was Roy F. Bergengren (1880–1955), a young lawyer who was to become the leader of the credit union movement in the United States. On July 1, 1921, Filene and Bergengren set up the Credit Union National Extension Bureau under an agreement that Filene would provide the money, and Bergengren devote his full time, to the Bureau.

Here, in Bergengren's words taken from his book *CUNA Emerges* (1935), pp. 23–25, is the story of that beginning:

I well recall the first day.

Into an empty office we moved an empty desk, an empty file, an empty chair and an old typewriter. I then sat in the empty chair at the empty desk and wondered how one went about the nationalization of cooperative credit.

That was fourteen years ago.

As had already been noted we had four workable credit union laws and 190 credit unions. We agreed on the first day that the Bureau had four objectives, and these objectives have never been changed or amended. We have been obliged during the years to make many detours; there is no getting to worth while objectives in a straight line, for human nature supplies too many twists in the road, too many mires, too many interruptions. Our first objective was to make it possible, by adequate legislation, to organize credit unions anywhere in the United States and the territorial possessions thereof. Second, we appreciated the need for a vast experimentation with the credit union plan, its complete Americanization and that there would be a great initial inertia to overcome, including particularly the quite erroneous, but then generally accepted theory that the American people would not take to cooperative effort. This second objective involved the organization of individual credit unions until the plan had been popularized and methods of credit union mass production had evolved.

The third objective looked forward to permanent, self sustaining state leagues of credit unions which would, in each state, take over the local direction of credit union development. Finally, it was our purpose, from the beginning to organize the Credit Union National Association as a national union of the credit unions as soon as the credit unions were numerous enough and had sufficient capital to warrant such action, and to turn over to the Association, when organized, the permanent direction of the cooperative credit movement in the United States. We appreciated, of course, that there would be other essential phases of our program—publicity, education, protection of credit unions from taxation and unjust laws, and, *above all, the business of finding men and educating and developing men to whom the permanent conduct of the credit union movement could be safely transferred.*[1]

By 1934, all of the objectives had been reached. Credit unions could be organized under state law in 41 of the then 48 states and the District of Columbia. The biggest legislative hurdle of all, a federal law which permitted organization of federal credit unions anywhere in the United States or its territories, was surmounted in 1934 by the enactment of Senate Bill 1639 by the 73rd Congress. Over 3,000 credit unions were operating among all kinds of groups, and mass-production techniques had been perfected. Thirty-five state leagues were functioning. And finally in a memorable 5-day meeting at Estes Park, Colorado, 52 credit union leaders from 22 states held a constitutional convention to form a national union. On August 10, 1934, they signed the constitution and bylaws of the Credit Union National Association.

At the first meeting of the national board of directors in January of the following year, Edward A. Filene was elected president of the new national association and Roy F. Bergengren was chosen managing director. Madison, Wisconsin, was designated the official headquarters. On March 1, 1935, the affairs of the extension bureau were transferred to the Credit Union National Association. An era of dedicated trail-breaking had come to an end. Credit unions had been firmly established in the United States.

From 1934 we shall concentrate almost entirely on historical credit union events in the United States and Canada, not because the North American movement is pre-eminent—credit unions in other countries, especially Germany, are at least equally important—but because North American experience is interesting as an example of how credit unions develop

[1] Roy F. Bergengren, *CUNA Emerges* (CUNA, Madison, Wis., 1935), pp. 23–25.

in a country, and this experience may be instructive in countries where credit unions are just beginning. In the developing countries of Central and South America, Africa, Asia and the Far East, the influence of Canadian and United States credit unions has been notable in recent years. However, since there is no pattern that is so good that it should be copied slavishly, North American history should be reviewed for its weaknesses as well as its strengths.

The successes of North American credit unions are impressive: 20 million members in 27,000 credit unions have over 11 billion dollars in savings. In a cooperative that is noted for its individuality, credit union members have worked together remarkably well to build their institutions. And the credit unions themselves have proceeded with a unity of purpose, if not always a unity of method, to strengthen their state and provincial leagues, their national association and its affiliated business ventures. Lacking, however, a central bank or fund, the one essential link that could tie them together by mobilizing the full power of their money, they are far from being unified as a banking system.

In the sequence of events during the past 32 years there is abundant evidence that in a people's movement, education is power—and so is money. Whether the members of the credit unions will eventually educate themselves to the point where they can become the masters of their own money has yet to be seen.

The interpretation of events that follows may throw some light on the outcome. It concerns the role of three major institutions in the North American credit union movement—the United States Government, CUNA International, and CUNA Mutual Insurance Society—all of them very powerful, but each one limited in its abilities to forge the connecting link.

The Federal Credit Union Act

Fully as important as the organization of CUNA in 1934 was the crowning legislative achievement of that year, passage of the Federal Credit Union Act sponsored by Senator Morris Sheppard and Congressman Wright Patman, and signed into law by President Franklin Delano Roosevelt on June 26, 1934.

This legislation brought credit unions within the reach of everyone in the United States and its possessions. But it was unmistakably a small-loans statute with restrictive connotations of far-reaching significance and it did much to build the movement and to mold it in this way.

In those states where inertia or antagonism of a state banking authority could thwart applicants for a state credit union charter, the thrust of the organization program had been blunted. Now there was a way around these obstacles. Bergengren predicted that the number of federal credit unions might well surpass the state credit unions within a few years. While this was long delayed because of general preference for more liberal state charters, the federal law gave tremendous support to the organization of credit unions everywhere in the United States, and in Canada as well. In the next seven years the total number of credit unions in North America more than doubled.

The United States government was now actively promoting credit unions. One state, Wisconsin, had hired a paid organizer who had shown what could be done in a short time with concentrated effort. Now the Credit Union Section, as the new United States government agency was called, with a modest appropriation and small staff—but with more money and staff than CUNA could command—took the leadership and the movement took on new life, and new directions. The Federal Credit Union Act was to shape the concepts of credit union service more than anyone then realized. The movement was to feel the driving power of the United States government for expansion of credit union activity, and the full weight of its opposition to any change in the small-loan configuration of the federal credit unions.

To understand what has happened to the credit union movement in the United States we must look to the early state credit union laws that had preceded the federal law, and to events that followed the enactment of the federal law.

The state laws were not always consistent with each other, nor were they always skillfully written. What went into the legislative hopper did not always resemble too closely what finally came out as law. Nevertheless, the concept of credit union service was still flexible and most of these laws expressed the will of the people to form credit unions that would enable them to save their money together for any kind of loan or other financial services they might need.

The early credit unionists were greatly influenced by Raiffeisen. Obviously their thinking was influenced by the depression that had started in 1929 and most of them never expected to see organizations with much money. But they were not in principle devoted to the small-loan concept. In the formative period of state legislation there was a clear-cut intention to finance homes and small businesses as many state credit unions still do. Credit unions were to function along the lines of the Raiffeisen societies, providing their members with the kind of financial assistance they needed without regard to so-called consumer loans or any other specific kind of loan. The only such reference as in the Raiffeisen societies was the rule that small loans would be given preference when any question arose over the availability of funds to make loans.

As late as 1935 Bergengren was still writing of people's banks and many of the credit union pioneers of that day hoped to see a people's banking system gradually evolve. Most of the state laws provided for deposit accounts. These accounts were being used in the *caisses populaires* of Quebec to give checking service, although in the United States then as today only the commercial banks could provide this service to depositors.

Was the banks' monopoly to be broken some day by the credit unions? In *CUNA Emerges* Bergengren tackles the questions of credit unions' competing with commercial banks for savings and deposits and he says:

Incidentally, even if credit unions took money from other banks (which they clearly do not, as each credit union does its business with a bank) the rightness or wrongness of the process would not depend on the resulting effect on the bank *but on the single test of whether or not the individual whose money is in question, is served better one way or the other.*

In 1965 Representative Wright Patman of Texas, one of the original sponsors of the Federal Credit Union Act and a strong supporter of credit union causes ever since, introduced a bill in the Congress of the United States to permit federal credit unions to provide deposits accounts and checking services for their members.

The sponsors of the Federal Credit Union Act in 1934 had to overcome not only the anticipated opposition of commercial interests, but also that of powerful agencies within the federal government who had little faith in a people's banking system run by amateurs. Having just witnessed the total collapse of the nation's commercial-banking system in which thousands of banks had to close and billions of dollars were lost, under the management of eminent professional bankers, and still grappling with the problems of that debacle, they were more interested in patching up and reforming that system than they were in opening the door to a people's bank that would be run by amateurs. To get their approval, the proposed credit union law had to fit into the overall pattern of the banking system.

The rejuvenated banks, restored to respectability with a deposit-insurance program, were to become the "department stores" of the financial system with sole powers to offer checking accounts and wide authority—expanded in later years—to provide almost every conceivable type of service. Other financial institutions were to be highly specialized. Credit unions would fit into the small-loan category. Although they had come through the years of bank closing almost unscathed, they were to receive the same strict government supervision as the banks. These demands were conceded to clear the legislation in the final days of the legislative session.

Another concession was to prove even more limiting. The provision for a network of central credit unions which would enable individual credit unions to bank their surplus funds together, and create a system for their mutual strength, was sacrificed to appease the opposition. Central bank institutions for the Raiffeisen societies and the Canadian *caisses populaires* had proved successful, in fact essential to their growth and stabilization. In the United States the Federal Reserve System had been a major achievement for the commercial banks in 1913, and the principle of central banking was being extended to other financial institutions during the early 1930's. Credit unions were to remain as individual units, isolated from each other financially, at the complete mercy of the commercial banking system or the federal government in times of financial need.

In winning the day for a Federal Credit Union Act, the credit union movement lost a major battle.

Instead of laying the foundations for development of a cooperative people's banking system, the movement began to build on a narrow, small-loan framework. Today as in 1934 credit unions of the United States are units in a program. Although that program has succeeded beyond the hopes of the planners, credit unions have no way to pool their financial resources, except through stabilization programs of their leagues which are seriously limited or in a very few cases through central credit unions which cannot function as reserve institutions and are also isolated from each other. Most of the central credit unions in existence are more involved with lending to credit union officials than with credit union interlending.

Role of the Bureau of Federal Credit Unions

From the first days of the government-subsidized Credit Union Section with its small staff in the Farm Credit Administration which first administered the Federal Credit Union Act, up to the present time when the Bureau of Federal Credit Unions with its several hundreds of employees is fully supported by supervision and examination fees, the government supervisory authority has set an example of dedication and efficiency. It is interesting to conjecture what directions the credit union movement might have taken if the United States Congress had insisted on a less restrictive law.

Up to 1953 the Bureau of Federal Credit Unions depended on U.S. treasury funds for at least a part of its support, but in 1953 the bureau became fully self-supporting from examination and supervision fees. Contrasted with other agencies that are not so well insulated from pressures of congressmen and their constituents, the bureau has had a free hand to regulate federal credit unions, and this regulation with few exceptions has followed the restrictive pattern of the law itself. It has also had a strong influence on the entire North American credit union movement, including the supervisory authorities of the states and provinces, who respect the technical competence of the United States government agency.

The original law in 1934 limited the amount of an unsecured loan, character of the borrower being the only security, to $50.00. Successive amendments to the law in the next 22 years raised this amount to $750.00, each increase having been agreed to by the bureau, but these increases did little more than maintain a parity with the rise of the United States economy. It was not until 1949 that the maturity period for loans was increased from two to three years, again keeping pace with the competition of other consumer-lending agencies that were finding it necessary to stretch the payment period for people who wanted to buy new cars coming on the market at sharply increased prices. When the Federal Credit Union Act was rewritten in 1959, one of the changes desired by the credit union movement was a further extension of the loan-maturity period to five years. The bureau would not agree to this until a proviso was included to make all loan maturities subject to bureau regulation. The traditional and fundamental concepts of self-management and self-responsibility in the most vital area of credit union operations, loans to members, were surrendered.

Rules and regulations now govern every conceivable aspect of federal credit union management. Page upon page of instructions keep elected officials and employees well inside the small-loan limitations, and warning signals are quickly raised if a credit union ventures to make a loan that approaches the legal limits.

With both federal and state supervisory authorities putting their prestige and power behind the small-loan concept, most credit unions find little reason to concern themselves with other ways to lend their money. Moreover, small-loan lending is lucrative; it is respectable; and it is safe. The fear of government criticism is much reduced when experimentation and risk-taking are eliminated. The search for new kinds of services, new ways to use the hundreds of millions of dollars of surplus funds that are piling up in North American credit unions, becomes a hazard instead of a challenge. Supervisory-agency criticism discourages even the most avid volunteers who do not depend on credit union jobs for their livelihood. It is a much more serious deterrent to career workers. When the elected officials sense that new services are needed which entail larger loans they are reluctant to dispute the government examiner's firm view that large loans are dangerous, and career managers whose record is often judged by their government examination report do not find it easy to take a stand that may earn them nothing but criticism.

Without a central system, through which to place their surplus funds in other productive investment that would directly benefit their members, all too often the credit unions turn to those permitted investments that pay the highest rates of interest. Unthinkingly, they may be financing institutions which earn a high return by exploitation of a community far removed from the credit union whose money makes it possible. The Michigan Credit Union League warned its member credit unions in 1964 that "High interest rates in California [paid by savings and loan associations] go hand-in-hand with higher costs to home borrowers." [1]

Relations between the bureau and federal credit unions are conducted in a dignified but paternalistic manner that increasingly places the government in the role of a federal regulatory agency which substitutes government fiat for the authority of the credit union members. In the large credit unions especially management answers to the government more than to the members who own the credit union. This is a consequence of members' abrogating their responsibilities, and government's willingness to assume these responsibilities for the sake of efficient operation. Given these conditions members cannot control their own money.

Usually if a question of judgment arises where the members might express their wishes in regard to activities of their credit union, there is a strict interpretation by the bureau of the "incidental powers" of federal credit unions, the only powers which are not specifically spelled out in the tightly

[1] *Contact*, October 1964, Vol. 13, No. 9.

worded law. Traditionally, the Federal Credit Union Act has been strictly interpreted to give federal credit unions only those powers spelled out in the law. Even the incidental-power clause which could provide some degree of flexibility has been narrowly construed.

Thus in 1964 it was ruled that members of a federal credit union could not authorize their credit union to obtain group life insurance for them through their league-owned insurance company. Similarly, it was ruled that federal credit unions could not advance dues to their league (presumably to help provide themselves with services through that league). Since there is no specific provision in the law to authorize these efforts at cooperation within credit unions and among credit unions, the only recourse available to those who disagree with rulings such as these is through expensive administrative and judicial appeals. Few credit unions have ventured to match their strength with the government in such a contest.

In its relations with the organized movement, the bureau on occasion has taken the initiative to mobilize support for legislation that would strengthen the financial stability of credit unions. Studies have been published to show the need for a central credit union system. In 1955 and 1956 the economic report of the President carried recommendations for a share-insurance program modeled along the lines of the government deposit-insurance plan for banks and savings-and-loans associations.

Despite the network of rules and regulations that govern federal credit unions, losses from large embezzlements and mismanagement have proved embarrassing at times. Equally troublesome have been the liquidations of credit unions whose members have been thrown out of work by a plant closing or, more frequent in recent years, the closing of a large defense establishment.

The solution of government share insurance has appealed to the bureau and to some segments of the organized movement, but the majority's resistance to more government regulation has blocked legislative proposals for share insurance and left the bureau to work out individual solutions as the various problems arise. This has led to some strong differences of opinion with individual state leagues which have undertaken to represent member credit unions in trouble with the government. Out of these differences has come a better understanding by leagues of the government's headaches in dealing with distressed credit unions, and an acceptance by the bureau of the leagues' growing effectiveness in helping their member credit unions to extricate themselves from their difficulties.

Stabilization programs of the leagues have demonstrated the power of cooperation and individual initiative. However, they depend on flexibility and resourcefulness to make limited amounts of money suffice for the orderly collection of members' loans, and the restoration of morale in credit unions that have been forced to liquidate or those in which members' confidence has been shaken by mismanagement or dishonesty losses. Government supervisory agencies accustomed to working along established lines of procedure, and with little flexibility in their own operations, find it difficult to accept the opposite approach that shuns rules and regulations in favor of versatility. Reluctantly at first, but with good grace, the bureau has begun to recognize the fact that the credit union movement is determined to utilize the growing stockpile of stabilization experience in many states to lay the foundation for a national program of credit union share protection dependent not on government supervision or financing but on the pooling of reserves, technical skills and leadership which exist in the credit unions themselves.

In 1964, at the initiative of the bureau, the Federal Credit Union Act was amended to give federal credit unions the right to invest in other federal cooperative agencies and other corporations wholly owned by the government. This was the first substantive expansion of investment powers for federal credit unions since 1937, and it could make the next step easier in moving toward a credit union-owned, movement-controlled federal cooperative agency which could combine the functions of central banking and share protection, using the interlending experience of central credit unions and the techniques of stabilization programs in credit union rescue operations.

In its research, statistics, and other technical programs the bureau has attempted to keep in step with the credit unions it serves. The bureau's special projects to encourage credit unions among low-income groups and to assist in the international-aid programs of the United States, attest to its continuing importance as a source of strength for the entire credit union movement.

Given a more liberal law to administer, along the lines of recent proposals in the Patman bill to permit checking-deposit accounts, or given the challenge of responsibilities for using its competent staff in a central-fund-share insurance plan, the bureau could again become a leader in new developments as it was thirty years ago.

CUNA International and CUNA Mutual Insurance Society

Prior to 1945 the credit union movement was usually written-off by its competitors as a nonentity of well-meaning but unskilled amateurs who had ventured into an area of finance where they were making no great impact. After 1945 when the postwar boom carried the movement to billion-dollar totals, competitors became troubled by the amount of money being handled by the "amateur bankers" but no more so than the credit union movement itself. As we have seen, the federal government felt justified in breaking the traditional barriers between supervision and management when individual credit unions began to deal in millions of dollars. Other traditions had to give way in the face of changes in the economic and social conditions of the postwar period, and in the process leaders of the movement often found themselves in disagreement.

Each proposed change in the structure or services of the movement, of the credit unions, the leagues and the national organizations, raised a troublesome question: would it be a departure from the *philosophy* of the credit union movement? The expressions of credit union philosophy that had come down from the writings of Raiffeisen, Desjardins, Filene and Bergengren were understandably not identical but they emphasized the brotherhood of man and the importance of man's control over his own money, through democratic institutions which gave full recognition to the dignity, the individual worth and the creativity of each human being. The application of these fundamentals to specific activities of the credit unions, the leagues and the national organizations had to be determined in relation to a changing world. Philosophy? Tradition? Custom? Most credit union leaders recognized the inevitability of change. They were willing to change their customs, reluctant to abandon their traditions and opposed to any change in their philosophy. But the issues came up sharply and insistently with each successful development of business services by credit unions and their organizations which had to compete in a business world that had little regard for credit union philosophy.

Although Filene's generosity had provided financial security for CUNA since its inception in 1934, the first elected leaders of CUNA were keenly aware that they had to find a good formula for self-support, one that would work on a long-range basis. It seemed only natural and certainly more economical to operate the parent organization, CUNA, together with its insurance society and supply branch under the same management, with members of the CUNA board of directors holding the elective positions in all three organizations. They debated financing plans from two different points of view. Some contended that CUNA should be supported by a system of voluntary dues, and that any earnings from the insurance, supply or other business activities should be returned to the leagues and the credit unions. Others believed that, although dues might be necessary to get CUNA started, all earnings from business activities should revert to CUNA and eventually these earnings should be used to eliminate dues altogether. The first viewpoint prevailed. CUNA and the leagues have always subsisted on voluntary dues.

The first board of directors may have foreseen in 1935 that frictions would result if CUNA had to rely on its business subsidiaries for financial support. What they did not foresee was that after 20 years CUNA would be struggling to match the services provided by some of its member leagues, while its insurance society would be powerful enough to split off from its parent organization and threaten to usurp CUNA's role as the national organization of the United States credit union movement.

In 1940 CUNA became fully self-supporting. Bergengren and a small staff managed to divide their time among the parent body and its two affiliates, always building on the traditions of unity. Bergengren was retired in 1945, handing over to his successor Thomas W. Doig the difficult job of holding CUNA and CUNA Mutual together. During the next ten years it became harder and harder to reconcile the needs of the parent and its business offspring. Both organizations had to adjust to the demands of large credit unions and powerful state leagues. During World War II over a thousand credit unions had liquidated; this sharpened the instincts for self-survival in the two major institutions since their entire existence depended on a growing number of credit unions. After the war, contrary to pessimistic forecasts of a business recession, the United States and Canadian economies surged to unprecedented heights and the credit union mood changed from one of retrenchment to one of unlimited expansion. CUNA and CUNA Mutual grew stronger as the credit unions prospered, but not evenly in relation to each other. This unevenness in growth led to differences that broadened and deepened.

At first the disputes resulted from the simple fact that the parent body found it increasingly difficult to steer its insurance subsidiary, which had become financially the stronger of the two. Unlike the supply cooperative which progressed gradually while doing a modest business with the credit unions, the insurance society measured its growth in the millions of dollars each year as credit union shares and loans mounted up. Clearly the insurance business was heading for success and could count on big money for its operations compared to that realized from CUNA's limited dues. In 1949 CUNA Mutual already had coverage of over $400 million and an annual payroll of $157,000 while the total income of CUNA was just over $140,000.

And as the millions multiplied, other insurance companies began to compete for the lucrative business of insuring credit unions. CUNA and the leagues to which it looked for support

had a direct interest in urging credit unions to put movement loyalty above lower operating costs, but they felt equally
justified in exercising control over CUNA Mutual to keep the
insurance costs as low as possible. The close ties between
CUNA and CUNA Mutual became progressively weakened
as the insurance society pursued its own course. The break
became inevitable with Doig's failing health and his death in
1955. Tension between leaders of the two organizations
reached a breaking point over the choice of his successor and
the CUNA Mutual board set up its own management in open
defiance of CUNA. Bergengren, to many the symbol of traditional unity, died in that same year.

With separate management, CUNA and CUNA Mutual
each built a faction led by the elected officials and top staff
who worked as hard to maintain positions of leadership in
the organized movement as they did to carry on their service
functions.

Since 1955 both CUNA and CUNA Mutual have moved
decisively to exert their influence in the organized movement.
Many of the issues debated within the movement since 1955
have been decided on the basis of the league delegates' alle-
giance to one organization or the other. With many of CUNA's
key employees in the CUNA Mutual camp after 1955, it was
inevitable that the differences among the elected officials
would spill over into the staff. And even more—influential
leaders from the entire credit union movement were caught
up in the controversies that swirled around the personalities
involved in the conflict which had spread beyond the boundaries of North America. Some of the issues were of worldwide
interest, bringing to the surface such latent differences as that
between supporters of official affiliation with the cooperative
movement (generally from the CUNA faction) and others
who opposed such affiliation, usually identified with the
CUNA Mutual faction.

The contest widened into a battle for control over CUNA
itself, but as the heat of personal feelings died down it became evident that most credit union grassroots leaders had
accepted the fact that the insurance society would no longer
be under the control of CUNA, just as neither would CUNA

Mutual be permitted to extend its political power by dominating CUNA. The 1965 candidates for officers' positions on the CUNA International board were elected without a contest.

In both factions there was genuine concern for the preservation and advancement of an enterprise—be it CUNA or CUNA Mutual—to which many people have selflessly devoted themselves, a cause for which they could fight with self-righteous conviction. Personal ambitions, human weaknesses, vested interests and the power that goes with money all played a part in the struggle. But the main reasons were economic.

The second world war and Regulation W of the Federal Reserve Board which curbed consumer credit cut back the business in group-loan and savings insurance with a three-edged sword. Credit union organization during wartime could not keep pace with the attrition from liquidating credit unions. Members' savings were diverted from credit union shares to war bonds, and loans to members fell off drastically as credit unions conscientiously complied with wartime credit regulations. With the decline in shares and loans from these three causes, CUNA Mutual's coverage dropped precipitately. This brought a determination to get more individual policies (always a goal of the society), and it also brought CUNA Mutual face to face with the inescapable fact that credit unions had to be organized for business reasons as well as altruistic reasons, as long as the main source of its business was from group credit union policies and not from individual polices. A strong field staff to sell insurance and promote credit unions seemed to the society to be the logical answer, but it was viewed quite differently by CUNA and the leagues.

Many of the leagues opposed CUNA Mutual's decision to create a separate field force. Not only would this detract from the cost advantages of the society, they reasoned, it also could be the means of building a rival organization to CUNA. At the very least it broke all the traditions of the unified movement they had helped to build. But other leagues supported changes which management of the society called essential, in some cases because having so few services to offer they depended on the insurance services to attract and hold member credit unions. They also relied on the society's ability to help them buy time while they strengthened themselves. One of the best selling points for CUNA Mutual's services, insofar as the leagues were concerned, was the time-honored underwriting rule that league membership was required before a credit union could buy CUNA Mutual's insurance policies; and these policies would be cancelled if the credit union should decide to terminate its league membership. When this protection proved insufficient, CUNA Mutual found other ways to help the leagues while fortifying itself for competitive onslaughts. The field force became part of an agency system, and a network of district field offices marked CUNA Mutual's independent course. With each step it severed traditional relations with the leagues and CUNA, to adjust to economic pressures in the competition for insurance business.

Economic forces were at work in the credit unions, too. For many years loan protection and life-savings insurance premiums have been the second highest expense for most credit unions. As credit unions grew into sizeable organizations and adopted a more critical attitude toward their business operations, this heretofore unquestioned expense came under scrutiny, and other insurance companies which had never shown any interest in credit union business now began to pursue it with zeal. These outsiders began successfully to invade the credit union preserve of CUNA Mutual, offering substantial premium reductions to large credit unions and especially to those with a favorable loss experience. The idea was new to credit unions, but well accepted among insurance companies —adjust the price of the insurance to the risk.

No one in credit union circles would have dared to suggest—as the competitive companies were now doing—that there might be some logic in adjusting insurance rates to the risks of insuring credit unions according to their loss experience. Here was a real dilemma. The tradition had always been share and share alike in the losses and in the dividends. This followed credit union philosophy, but in maintaining the tradition there was the hazard of compounding the problem of CUNA Mutual and the credit unions which remained loyal to their society. Added to the loss of the sizeable premiums paid by some of the largest credit unions would be the heavier concentration of risks in the high-loss credit unions whose business was shunned by the profit-seeking companies. CUNA Mutual's decision to hold to its traditional policy resolved the dilemma but at the cost of hundreds of millions of dollars of coverage, and some years later that decison had to be reversed quietly with the issuance of insurance policies patterned on those of competitive companies.

When the larger member credit unions began to listen to proposals from other insurance companies, the effect on the leagues was immediate and painful. They feared the loss of dues from some of their largest supporters, and with good reason. The CUNA Mutual underwriting rule offered little protection for the league, when credit unions discovered that they could get the same insurance at lower rates whether or not they belonged to the league. More and more of them made it clear that if they decided to remain with the league they would do so on the basis of the league's services alone, and they would expect the league's help in getting insurance at low cost. This had a healthy effect on leagues that had allowed their services to lag, but it brought more confrontations with the insurance society.

CUNA Mutual's management was not always receptive to pleas from the leagues for more realistic premium rates to meet the competition—and certainly not to their demands— if the leaders of those leagues were identified with the pro-CUNA instead of the pro-CUNA Mutual faction of the movement.

In 1958 the Michigan Credit Union League, urged on by a number of its large member credit unions, pressed CUNA Mutual for a change in its premium structure. Unable to get satisfaction, the league membership voted at a special meeting in December 1958 to acquire a company which would provide insurance to meet the needs of Michigan credit unions. Within six years the league's insurance company which adopted a modified form of loss experience rate structure and pioneered a new type of life insurance policy—the family-group plan more suited to the protection of young families—

was able to claim over $2 billion of coverage in member credit unions, while CUNA Mutual lost almost all of its business in Michigan.

To have a league audacious enough and strong enough to challenge CUNA Mutual was a shocking experience for the credit union movement, but it revealed as nothing else could that even a traditionally sheltered, large and powerful affiliate of the movement, could not be protected from the economic facts of life. There was another jarring awakener for all the national bodies—an individual league had demonstrated its ability to win a contest with one of the national organizations. Leagues had come into their own as a power on the national scene.

The leagues had suffered perhaps more than either of the national organizations through the World War II period, but in the process they had attracted leaders who were toughened on hard times and determined to build as never before once the war was ended. Some of these leaders were died-in-the-wool cooperators. During the war years they had held their leagues together by dint of supreme effort and, with the quickening of credit union activity after the war, they saw the potential for building organizations that could finally take up the longstanding challenges through education, training, promotion and technical advances extending even to establishment of a central credit union bank—all of which could transform the credit unions into a dynamic financial system representing millions of Americans in the new economy of abundance. To them, credit union philosophy was the thread that ran continuously through all their endeavors and plans; it was just as viable for large credit unions as for small ones.

Their convictions were strengthened by the support of a whole new contingent of leaders who had been attracted to the credit movement by its growing successes in the postwar years. When CUNA Mutual showed signs of embarking on an independent course with a well-financed program and a large field staff, the implications did not escape them. They were determined that if they could not prevent the insurance affiliate from going its own way at least they would not surrender their control of the national association. In 1954, and the national elections thereafter, they consolidated their position in CUNA.

Long before the break with CUNA, leaders of CUNA Mutual tried to plan for some way to assure democratic control of their society. They had not far to look for the experience of other mutual insurance companies in America, which had gone in the opposite direction. Was there any assurance that CUNA Mutual would be different from the other mutuals with their self-perpetuating boards of directors and management?

After six years of debate a proposal was made in the late 40's to convert the society into a stock company, whose ownership would be vested in the movement, but this failed to win majority support partly because of the insuperable legal obstacles. Instead, area meetings of policy owners were inaugurated to give some expression to the views of the thousands of owners who could not physically attend the biennial meetings and elections of the society. In 1957 the society initiated a plan that was proving successful in another mutual company, to get membership participation through policyowner representatives meetings. The POR program continues to provide a sounding board for management policies in the United States and Canada, and it gives the policyowners a forum for discussion, but insofar as the law is concerned nothing but discussion can come from POR meetings unless the board of directors so desires.

When in 1955 the CUNA Mutual board of directors asserted their right, indeed their obligation, to govern the insurance society as an independent organization to comply with the law, they were invoking powers that others before them in other mutual insurance companies had found to be necessary for getting and keeping control of a big insurance business. When billions of dollars are involved—in 1965 coverage exceeded $9.7 billion—there must be protection for the policyowners. To this end the laws governing mutual insurance societies provide another kind of protection—protection of the incumbent officials and management from disruption and change. Continuity of management is assured.

In the leagues just the opposite is true. Debate, active participation by voting delegates, and even controversy are the lifeblood of a league. Being voluntary organizations founded on democratic principles, they have the strengths and weaknesses of democracies. Member credit unions often are loyal to a league whose performance leaves much to be desired, and leagues will support the apex organization even when they are heartily dissatisfied with its administration.

On the other hand, credit unions can exist without league membership no matter how good the services of the league may be, or how reasonable the dues. As the credit unions get larger they are less responsive to the call of the group. There is no penalty for dropping out of a league and failing to pay dues; readmittance is easily obtained. Delegates to league meetings are not reluctant to express their convictions on matters that are not within the specialized areas of business activity, and many league board members have little regard for the continuity of their paid staff. Disruptions and changes in league management are as well accepted as is continuity in the mutual insurance society.

In 1957 CUNA, CUNA Mutual, CUNA Supply Cooperative and leagues adopted a code that was supposed to delineate the respective areas of the separate organizations. Notwithstanding, CUNA Mutual has continued to press ahead into areas of organization, promotion and education designed to organize and create new credit unions, build membership and increase shares and loans, which strictly speaking are not insurance activities. One of the features of the new program is the offer by CUNA Mutual to provide and pay all the salary and travel expenses of one or more field representatives for leagues which support the CUNA Mutual programs, including those in some of the developing countries. Numerous leagues have accepted this help, and this has engendered debates of new intensity.

Most of the leagues, however, have generally supported CUNA up to now in its resistance to any incursion by CUNA Mutual into areas that traditionally have been reserved to themselves. This has hardly discouraged the insurance society —if anything, it has spurred actions to build the kind of organization management believes is essential. Whenever possible CUNA Mutual has located its field offices in the buildings of friendly leagues, and by providing them with paid staff it is cementing relations with more than ideological binders. Despite opposition within the movement, and competition, it has succeeded in retaining official recognition as the insurance arm of the movement for loan protection and life-savings insurance business. CUNA Mutual claims that 9 out of 10 credit unions use its loan-protection coverage. There is a growing realization that CUMIS Insurance Society, its subsidiary in the casualty insurance field, may soon win similar recognition by becoming the carrier of surety bonds for credit unions. The stakes are a multi-million dollar business that another company which contracts with CUNA International has built up over a period of many years.

Hope for Unity

If it be true that organizations invariably reflect the people who belong to them and the leaders they elect, the North American credit union movement gives us a picture of human beings who are dedicated, foresighted and idealistic—also shrewd and cognizant of their own self-interests. These people, despite their differences and preoccupation with insurance, have accomplished much for others to emulate.

CUNA International has successfully transformed itself from a small national association into an organization representing 77 credit union leagues in 70 countries around the world. It is a center for legislative, educational, technical and promotional efforts that are gaining members, money and prestige for credit unions everywhere. It is identified with the civic groups that are vocal in the campaign for consumer protection. The president of CUNA International is among the most active advocates of the consumers council appointed by the President of the United States, and increasingly the council's activities are centered around discussion groups brought together by the credit union leagues. Further broadening its organization program, CUNA invested $50,000 in 1964 to help low-income groups in the United States bring credit union service to those who need it most. The pace of organization has slowed considerably from that of the 1930's or the postwar 40's, but the movement is still growing in numbers of individual members—over a million members yearly for the past several years.

The international organization was built on geographical leagues yet it has shown the ability to accommodate special-interest groups of credit unions, those of the United States defense forces, which have found it necessary to associate in a separate organization that transcends the geographical boundaries of the leagues. In recognizing the Defense Credit Unions Council, CUNA has opened up the possibilities of an entirely new way of weaving the movement together. Since 1962 when the defense council was organized with an executive secretary on CUNA's staff, innumerable problems of armed forces credit unions have been overcome with the help of the entire CUNA International organization, binding them closer to the organized movement than league affiliation alone could have done.

For many years the National Association of Managing Directors (NAMD)—since 1964 known as the International Association of Managing Directors—made up of league personnel, was the only professional society for career workers in the movement. It had won respect for being concerned as much with the welfare of all those associated with the movement as for its own members, but it could not represent the credit union managers who were elected to the league boards. In 1961 CUNA staff working with the leagues designed a new program, CUNA Executive Services (CUES) to provide management training and other specialized technical services for the career managers to equip them for their professional duties in credit unions that were growing larger, more complex in their operations and more concerned about the quality of their management in a competitive business world. The CUES Managers Society was founded in 1962 under a specially drawn agreement that keeps it under the umbrella of CUNA's sponsorship.

Starting in 1962 CUNA International has entered into contracts with the United States Agency for International Development and the United States Peace Corps to staff and administer programs of credit union development in other countries. The world extension program of CUNA has, since 1954, given help to people outside of North America who cannot get assistance from the government-to-government foreign-aid programs. Each year CUNA's budget includes a sizeable sum for world extension entirely apart from the government-financed activities, thus helping to assure that when and if the need arises CUNA can continue its own program independently. Of all the programs of CUNA, world extension is possibly the activity which has done more than anything else to bring admiration from many important observers in the world. Also it has helped more than anything else in the past ten years to unify the movement, because it gives recognition to the need and desire of most credit union members for a way to participate in the cause of international cooperation and world peace.

Stabilization programs originally pioneered by the Saskatchewan league in Canada, and the Michigan league in the United States, now function in many leagues including several outside of North America which have been helped to start by the CUNA International Stabilization Program. The purpose of stabilization is to assist credit unions to protect the value of their members' shares in the event of insolvency or liquidation. Most of the stabilization programs are funded through regular appropriations of league dues and, although the reserves they have built up are extremely limited, the leagues have managed to accomplish unusual feats by resourcefulness in their coordination of whatever staff, money and support are available in their communities. Flexibility is the guide to stabilization success, rather than rules, regulations or by-laws. Their accomplishments have given a new feeling of confidence to the leagues, and have stimulated thinking about the ability of the movement to unify itself economically and politically through a sharing of its reserves, its leadership and its technical facilities in some kind of central bank that combines the functions of interlending and stabilization.

The greatest test of economic strength, it has been said, is the ability "to disagree at all times yet hold fast together." Strong as they are, North American credit unions have a long way to go in mobilizing their total resources, and it is not likely that credit union members will permit disagreements to divert their attention for long from the search for fulfillment of their economic and social goals. Strangely enough they may find the directions they need in the experiments of credit unions just starting in other lands where poor people are financing homes and small businesses, instead of consumer goods.

And perhaps not so strange, the most exciting history of this people's movement may be made in those countries where adversity still drives the people to hold fast together.

BIBLIOGRAPHY

*Accounting Manual for Federal Credit Unions, Washington, D.C. Bureau of Federal Credit Unions, Department of Health, Education, and Welfare (July 1965) FCU 544.

*"All About Credit," Reprint from Changing Times, March 1963.

"Back Again—Out-of-State S'Ls," Contact. Detroit, Michigan Credit Union League, October 1964, p. 13.

*Bergengren, Roy F., CUNA Emerges. Madison, Wis., CUNA, 1935.

*Black, Robert P. and Harless, Doris E., Nonbank Financial Institutions, Federal Reserve Bank of Richmond, June 1965.

*Boyan, R. H., What Kind of Credit Society? Noumea, New Caledonia, South Pacific Commission, SPC Co-operatives Booklet No. 1, March 1961.

*Boyle, George, The Poor Man's Prayer. New York, Harper & Brothers, 1951.

Briefs. Madison, Wisconsin, CUNA Public Relations Department, CUNA International, Inc.

Bureau of Federal Credit Unions Bulletin. Washington, D.C., Department of Health, Education, and Welfare, April 1965.

*Clements, Muriel, By Their Bootstraps. Toronto, Vancouver, Clarke, Irwin & Company, Ltd., 1965.

"Consumers Gather in California," Credit Union Magazine. Madison, Wis., CUNA International, Inc., Vol. 31, No. 2.

Contact. Detroit, Michigan Credit Union League, Vol. 14, No. 10.

Co-op Report. Chicago, Cooperative League of the U.S.A., Vol. 14, No. 3.

Cooperatives U. S. A. 1963–1964. Chicago, Cooperative League of the U.S.A., 1965.

Credit Committee Ideas. Detroit, Education Department, Michigan Credit Union League, Vol. 1, No. 2, 3, 4, 5; Vol. 2, No. 2.

*Credit Manual for Federal Credit Unions. Washington, D.C., Bureau of Federal Credit Unions, Department of Health, Education and Welfare (Nov. 1959), FCU 548.

The Credit Union World Is Your World. Report of Board of Directors, CUNA International, Inc., 1965.

*Croteau, John T., *The Economics of the Credit Union*. Detroit, Wayne State University Press, 1963.
———— *The Federal Credit Union: Policy and Practice*. New York, Harper and Brothers, 1956.
"CU Membership Exceeds 16 Million," *Credit Union Magazine*. CUNA International, Inc., Vol. 30, No. 11.
"CUs Third Largest in Consumer Credit," *Credit Union Magazine*. CUNA International, Inc., Vol. 30, No. 11.
CUNA Mutual Memos. Madison, Wis., CUNA Mutual Insurance Society.
CUNA Mutual Newsletter. Madison, Wis., CUNA Mutual Insurance Society.
Dublin, Jack, *Central Banking, Stabilization and Share Insurance for Credit Unions*. (Study done for Michigan Credit Union League, Detroit, 1962.)
———— *How We Stabilize Credit Unions in Michigan*. (Address to Delegates, Massachusetts CUNA Association, Inc., April 9, 1960.)
———— *Internal Control of Credit Unions Through Analysis of Financial Statements*. (Paper presented at First CUNA Management Specialists Conference, Madison, Wis., December 1958.)
Federal Credit Union Program, Annual Report, 1964. Washington, D.C., Bureau of Federal Credit Unions, Department of Health, Education, and Welfare. FCU 561.
*Filene, Edward A., *Successful Living in This Machine Age*. New York, Simon and Schuster, 1932.
"Fighting the 'Juice Racket,'" *Credit Union Magazine*. CUNA International, Inc. Vol. 30, No. 1.
For Your Information. Madison, Wis., CUNA Public Relations Department, CUNA International, Inc.
"The Forum Plan," *Credit Union Magazine*. CUNA International, Inc., Vol. 30, No. 9.
*Giles, Richard Y., *Credit For The Millions*. New York, Harper & Brothers, 1951.
———— "Licensed Moneylenders," *The Bridge*. Credit Union National Association, January 1942.
The Great Credit Union Story. Madison, Wis., CUNA Mutual Insurance Society, 1965.
Guidelines. Detroit, Education Department, Michigan Credit Union League, 1965.
Guidelines for Credit Union Management. Detroit, Education Department, Michigan Credit Union League, November 1960.
Handbook for Federal Credit Unions. Washington, D.C., Bureau of Federal Credit Unions, Department of Health, Education, and Welfare, FCU 543 (Rev. 7-64).
Humphrey, James, "How Cooperative-type Insurance Companies Can Work with Other Co-Operatives." *Co-op Report*, Cooperative League of the U.S.A., Vol. 13, No. 10.
IMPACT. Madison, Wis., CUNA Supply Cooperative.
"Ingredients for a Successful Self-Sustaining Cooperative Housing Program." Washington, D.C., Study *Prepared for Agency for International Development*, Nov. 1965. (FCH Company, a subsidiary of the Foundation for Cooperative Housing.)
International Cooperative Alliance. Annual Report, July 1964.

International Credit Union Yearbook. Madison, Wis., CUNA International, Inc., 1964, 1965.

"The 'Juice Racket,'" *Everybody's Money.* Madison, Wis., CUNA International, Inc., Vol. 5, No. 1.

*Kallen, Horace M., *The Decline and Rise of the Consumer.* Chicago, Packard and Company, 1945.

*Margolius, Sidney, *A Guide to Consumer Credit.* Public Affairs Pamphlet No. 348, 1963.

——— *How to S-T-R-E-T-C-H Your M-O-N-E-Y.* Public Affairs Pamphlet No. 302, 1960.

McVoy, J. David, "Closing the Gap in Housing Through Cooperatives," *FCH News Briefs.* Washington, D.C., Foundation for Cooperative Housing, Vol. 11, No. 11.

"New Hire Purchase Regulation," *The Nationalist.* Dar es Salaam, Tanzania, Feb. 5, 1966.

Polner, Walter, *Attitudes of League Directors Toward Stabilization Plans and a Government Program of Share Insurance,* paper presented to CUNA Stabilization Committee, Madison, Wis., Credit Union National Association, 1963.

The Raiffeisen Organization in Western Germany. Bonn, Deutscher Raiffeisenverband E. V., 1959.

RE Statistical Bulletin. Madison, Wis., CUNA Research and Economics Department, CUNA International, Inc.

Rural Cooperatives in the Federal Republic of Germany. Bonn, Agricultural and Home Economics Evaluation and Information Service, Ministry of Food, Agriculture, and Forestry, 1961.

*Samuelson, Paul A., *Economics.* New York, McGraw-Hill Book Company, Inc., 1961.

"See Big Gains for 1965," *Credit Union Magazine.* CUNA International, Inc., Vol. 31, No. 1.

Statistical Yearbook. Detroit, Michigan Credit Union League, 1965.

"Steer Clear of 'Second Mortgage Broker' Racket," *Everybody's Money.* Madison, Wis., CUNA International, Inc., Vol. 5, No. 2.

Summary Report on League Stabilization Plans. Unpublished study, CUNA International, Inc., August 1961.

"30th Anniversary of the Federal Credit Unions," *Indicators,* Reprint, Nov. 1964. Washington, D.C., U. S. Department of Health, Education, and Welfare, Office of the Assistant Secretary (for Legislation).

Trends. CUNA Research and Economics Department, CUNA International, Inc. # 27 (December 8, 1965).

*Voorhis, Jerry, *American Cooperatives.* New York, Harper & Brothers, 1961.

——— *Credit Unions, Basic Cooperatives.* Chicago, Cooperative League of the U.S.A., 1959.

"When Credit Unions Borrow," *Credit Union Magazine.* Credit Union National Association, November 1963.

Wilson, Charles Morrow. *Common Sense Credit.* New York, The Devin-Adair Company, 1962.

World Book Encyclopedia, Chicago, Field Enterprises Educational Corporation, 1965.

*Suggested reading for students.

INDEX

Annual membership meeting, 55–56

Application for Loan, 116

Application for Membership, Signature Card, 115

Asset in bookkeeping, 104, 105, 108–09

Bergengren, Roy F., 148–49, 151, 152, 159, 162

Board of Directors, 53, 60, 68–69

Boerenbond, Belgian credit union, 142–43

Bookkeeping records, 103–04; stationery used, 113–18

Bookkeeping rules, double-entry system, 108–09

Bureau of Federal Credit Unions, 154–56

By Laws, 31, 34–35

Cash Payment Voucher, 114

Caisse Populaire de Levis, 146

Caisses populaires, 146–47, 152, 153

Cash Received Voucher, 113

Central Bank, 24, 139–40

Charter (or Formation) Meeting, 32–36; order of business, 34

Checkbook money, 131

Closing entries, 109–13; profit and loss, 109

Collections Sheet, 114

Common Bond, 29–30; occupational common bond, 29; residential common bond, 29–30; associational common bond, 30

Cooperative League of the U.S.A., 100

Cooperative Principle, 45–52

Cooperatives, types of, 51; relationship with each other, 51–52

Credit Committee, 53, 56, 60, 65, 67–68

Credit, need for, 130–40; as bookkeeping term, 105, 107, 108–09; high cost of, 132–34; shopping for, 135–39; measurement of price of, 137–39

Credit Union, definition, 9, 14, 26, 27–29, 141; purposes, 14; training ground for other cooperatives, 45–51; responsibility in cooperative development, 52; principles of operation, 119

Credit Union bank, reserve system, 24; central bank, 139–40, 150, 154, 156; central credit unions, 153; central credit union system, 157–58, 166, 171–72

Credit union movement, structure of, 84; statistical summary, 102

Credit Union National Extension Bureau, 148–49

Credit Union Section, U.S. Government, 151

The manuscript was edited by Ralph Busick. The book was designed by Donald Ross. The text type face is Mergenthaler Linotype's Caledonia designed by W. A. Dwiggins in 1937. The display face is Optima designed by Hermann Zapf for the Stempel Typefounders in 1958.

The book is printed on Allied Paper Company's Paperback Book paper. The hardcover edition is bound in Joanna Mills' Parchment Cloth; the papercover edition is bound in Riegel Paper Company's Carolina Cover. Manufactured in the United States of America.

The author, Jack Dublin, was educated at Denver University and George Washington University. Since 1937 he has served as a credit union technician and administrator, first with the United States government and later with the Michigan Credit Union League. In 1963 he began working on a credit union development project in East Africa sponsored by the credit union leagues of Saskatchewan and Michigan, and is now continuing this program in Tanzania, Kenya and Uganda under joint sponsorship of CUNA International, Inc. and the United States Agency for International Development. This book encompasses his experiences, drawn from the most active period of credit union growth in American history and the newest experiments of developing countries on the African continent who are just now beginning to build their own credit union movements.